SPANISH FOR ENGLISH SPEAKERS

The Essential Grammar within a full International Spanish Course

Alberto R. González

ISBN: 1530897165
ISBN-13: 978-1530897162

SPANISH FOR ENGLISH SPEAKERS
The essential grammar within a full International Spanish course

by Alberto R. González

ACKNOWLEDGMENTS

To my mother, Juliet, with all my love.

(May 14, 1928 – June 24, 2015)

To my parents, Francisco and Juliet, for all the education (both school and home) given; and to my brothers, Francisco and Juan, for always being exactly that: brothers.

To Fran and Noe, always a great inspiration and forever in my mind.

To all my cousins, uncles, aunts, and adopted relatives.

To all my students, in schools, colleges and institutes. You have proven through the years that educators really learn from their students.

...And talking about learning, thanks and regards to all my own teachers and professors, from school to university.

Thanks, God, for all your blessings in the Past, Present, and Future.

CONTENTS

ABOUT THE AUTHOR

Alberto González has taught Spanish and ESL (English as a Second Language) for years at an international language institute, and has tutored Spanish in college, as well as independently to college and high school English-speaking students.

His first language is Spanish, and throughout his experience providing Spanish language education to English speakers, and vice versa, he has focused his attention on integrating Spanish-English compared grammar into the learning process; always researching and developing effective learning material, from an international point of view, for those specific audiences.

He is also an English-Spanish translator and an article writer, who has provided translation services to different clients, has authored many articles in the cultural field, and is trained in English-Spanish interpretation.

ABOUT THE BOOK

Following the author's specific experience and interest, the intention of this book is to provide all the relevant material within a full International Spanish course, with the English-speaking students in mind; presenting all the essential grammar, from basic to advanced, plus additional information, hints and observations, in a simple and logical way with which the readers/students can build their language skills. All topics are explained in English, with examples in both Spanish and English.

Much of the information and the way it is presented are the direct result of the author's interaction with his students during learning sessions, taking as a great feedback their typical questions and struggles as English speakers approaching the Spanish language.

Based on the intention of keeping the complicated Spanish grammar as simple as possible (but without affecting the full coverage of relevant material for the overall mastering of this language), a couple of tenses have been intentionally not included due to not being so common or highly essential in modern International Spanish, and which normally do not appear in main textbooks used in colleges and schools in the USA, such as: "Pretérito Anterior Compuesto" and "Futuro Subjuntivo Simple / Compuesto".

This book is intended as a Supplemental Book; exercises and vocabulary are not provided. It makes an excellent "portable tutor" for the extensive material covered in an easy-to-carry size.

HISTORY BITS ABOUT THE SPANISH COLONIZATION

October 12, 1492: Marks the arrival of the Spanish Language and Christianity in the New World through an expedition led by Christopher Columbus on behalf of the Spanish Crown, making the Caribbean their first settled region.
– October 12 is known as Columbus Day, "Día de la Raza" (Day of the Race), and "Día de la Hispanidad" (Day of the Spanishness).

La Hispaniola/La Española (The Spanish One), today shared by Haiti and the Dominican Republic, was the name that the Spanish colonizers gave to the land where they established their first settlement in 1492, called "La Navidad" (Christmas), after exploring the shores of San Salvador (Bahamas) and Isla Juana (Cuba).

In 1493, a second trip led the Spaniards to San Juan Bautista (St. John the Baptist; now Puerto Rico), and completed the settlement in the Caribbean region after leaving settlers there and in Isla Juana (Cuba).

In 1494, Villa Isabela (north side of the Dominican Republic) became the first European village in the New World.

Santo Domingo, capital of the Dominican Republic, was founded in 1496; the oldest city in the New World, known as the Prime City of America*.

A third trip in 1498 drove the colonizers to Trinidad and Venezuela, in the Northern area of South America.

A fourth trip in 1502 led the Spaniards to Central America (Honduras).

In 1508, the Spaniards established their first village outside the Dominican Republic, Villa Caparra, in Puerto Rico.

In 1511, the first village in Cuba was established, Villa Baracoa.

Juan Ponce de León, after governing San Juan Bautista (Puerto Rico), departed to what he named "La Florida" (The Flowery One; now Florida, USA) in 1513.

The colonizers explored further West and arrived in Mexico (Veracruz), in 1519.

San Juan, capital of Puerto Rico, was founded as a city in 1521.

In 1522, Santiago (in Cuba) was declared a city.

The Spaniards established Saint Augustine (in Florida) in 1565; the oldest city in the USA.

*America = the American continent. Name given to the New World by the Spaniards in the late 1400s during their colonization process; and the way it is still known today in Spain and Latin America. One continent with three areas: North America (Canada, USA, and Mexico), Central America (from Guatemala to Panama) and South America (from Colombia and Venezuela to Chile and Argentina). A later version shows two continents: North America and South America.

THE SPANISH LANGUAGE IN THE NEW WORLD: AMERICA

The Arrival

According to historians, right when the Moorish 800-year presence in Spain ended in 1492, an Italian astronomer named Cristoforo Colombo (Christopher Columbus) was granted support by the Spanish Crown to explore new worlds. King Ferdinand and Queen Isabella sent Columbus along with three ships known as "La Niña", "La Pinta" and "La Santa María" to find the new lands he was sure existed.

It was October 12, 1492 when the expedition arrived in what today is the American Continent, exploring the shores of a couple of lands that were named "San Salvador" (today in the Bahamas) and "Isla Juana" (Cuba), and finally disembarking in what was named "La Hispaniola" (The Spanish One), now divided in two countries, Haiti to the west and the Dominican Republic to the east. After losing one of their ships on Christmas day some had to stay in La Hispaniola in what is the first European settlement in the New World, which they named "La Navidad" (Christmas) for obvious reasons. The others returned to Spain to bring the big news.

A second trip in 1493 drove the Spaniards to "San Juan Bautista" (St. John the Baptist; now Puerto Rico), leaving people there and in "Isla Juana" (Cuba), and in other found lands throughout the Caribbean region to complete the settlement.

In 1494, the first European village was established in America, "Villa Isabela" (Isabella's Village), known today as "Puerto Plata" (Silver Port), in the northern coast of the Dominican Republic. A little later, the Spaniards founded their first official city in 1496, Santo Domingo, known as America's Prime City and current capital of the Dominican Republic. At this point, the Spanish Crown had officially established in the Western Hemisphere a new language, Spanish; a new religion, Christianity (Catholic); and a new race, European.

Then, during a third trip in 1498 they explored the north side of South America (Trinidad and Venezuela), and later on arrived in Central America (Honduras) during a fourth trip in 1502. Years later, the Spaniards headed west and arrived in Mexico (Veracruz area) in 1519.

After Villa Isabela and Santo Domingo, other relevant villages and cities that were established at the beginning of this colonization process in the Caribbean region were "Villa Caparra" in 1508 and the City of San Juan in 1521, both in Puerto Rico, as well as "Villa Baracoa" in 1511 and the City of Santiago in 1522, these two in Cuba.

Juan Ponce de León, right after governing Puerto Rico, arrived in a land that he named "La Florida" (The Flowery One; today Florida, USA) in 1513.

Additionally, two other important events that occurred during the Spanish colonization process were the conquest of the Mayan Empire (Southwestern area of North America: Mexico) in 1521, and lastly, the conquest of the Incan Empire (Central area of South America: Peru) in 1532.

The racial mix that took place due to this colonization process, between this European civilization (the Spaniards), the different native inhabitant groups (Taínos, Mayas, Aztecs, Incas, etc.), and the subsequent addition of Africans, formed the Hispanic race.

On a final note, in 1565, the Spaniards founded "San Agustín" (Saint Augustine) in "La Florida", the oldest city in the United States.

The Development

Every country where the Spanish language was established during the Spanish colonization in America, has adopted, adapted and created new words, as well as a unique accent, based on each one of these nations' own experience and development. There are not two places where the exact same Spanish is spoken.

For more than 500 years after that Christopher Columbus's historical first voyage in 1492, the Spanish language in America has been influenced by many factors. As the Spaniards, far from their mainland Spain, spread and settled in many different areas like the Caribbean, Mexico, Central and South America, they encountered many different native inhabitants who they referred to as Indians, and then the addition of Africans completed the main ingredients that formed a new race in the New World. Every region that the Spaniards populated provided a unique combination of elements that years later produced a unique language result, like any other language in any other time.

A language, Spanish, newly established in a specific region like Mexico in North America, interacting with a specific native Indian group and combined with a specific African group, will be different compared to a very far away land like Chile or Argentina with their own combination of factors in the southern side of South America, and also compared to all the countries in between, passing through Central America. Another example is that the Spanish language in an area like the neighboring countries Ecuador, Peru and Bolivia, with a high native Indian presence since the colonization until the present day, produced Andean Spanish, which results to be different compared to the one in the first settled lands, the Caribbean area, with no native inhabitants during most of the post colonization times; therefore no direct indigenous language influence over the same period.

The Spanish (Castilian) language was born around the 1100s, in the midst of the Moorish presence in Spain; therefore, a vast number of Spanish words are from Arabic origin. A great way to see how much this language has changed through the years until the present time is by reviewing "El Cantar de Mío Cid", considered the first Castilian literary work (c.1200). It is very difficult for any Spanish speaker in present times, from any country, to understand it.

Reviewing manuscripts from the Spanish colonization times in the late 1400s and early 1500s would also reveal an obvious difference in spelling and vocabulary, in addition to verbs and pronouns arranged in a different order, although more understandable than "El Mío Cid". And even later than that, the finest Spanish literary work "Don Quijote de La Mancha" (early 1600), by Miguel de Cervantes, clearly proves that these same elements differ from our modern Spanish.

These few examples show some of the spelling differences in the Castilian language between Medieval and Present times (showing then→now): recebí→recibí, mesmo→mismo, della→de ella, dél→de él, desta→de esta, feridas→heridas, fermosa→hermosa, fuyan→huyan, among many others.

Try the same with English by comparing Shakespeare's literary work with current English. Then, try with any other language.

When countries are neighbors, their languages influence each other. But, besides this normal and logical fact, when a country grows and leads others, its language also affects that of other not-so-close countries, proportional to the level of expansion.

For instance, Latin influenced other languages due to the Roman Empire expansion, a fact that is evident when we see the etymology of words in any dictionary. Latin transformed into five major Romance (from Rome) languages: Romanian, Italian, French, Portuguese and Spanish. One of these successors of Latin, French, greatly influenced English and others during medieval times, when the Kingdom of France was a great power, to the point that around one third of the English vocabulary comes from French. Similarly, the Kingdom of England influenced many others with its language. Finally, in modern times, the English language has kept becoming more popular every day around the world, with an influence mostly coming from the United States during the last decades, and also from the communications technology revolution, mostly running in English. That explains why every Spanish speaking country, from Spain to anywhere in Latin America, counts with a great amount of words taken from English, "Anglicisms", even if they are geographically distant from English speaking countries. Today is less relevant to be in, or close to, the country of influence for a word crossover to happen.

It is quite interesting to see how a language is a mix of other languages, previous or contemporaneous. Here is a clear example of Latin incorporated into both Spanish and English, which many people have never realized: The calendar months. As we know them in English (capitalized) and in Spanish (not capitalized), they come from the Roman calendar in Latin (B.C.) and originally had ten months, starting on March (January and February were added later):

1. March (Roman deity) = Marzo
2. April (Roman deity) = Abril
3. May (Roman deity) = Mayo
4. June (Roman deity) = Junio
5. July (Julius Caesar) = Julio (Julio César)
6. August (Augustus Caesar) = Agosto (Augusto César)
7. September (seventh) = Septiembre (séptimo)
8. October (eighth) = Octubre (octavo)
9. November (ninth) = Noviembre (noveno)
10. December (tenth) = Diciembre (décimo)

Differences and Updates

As we all know, vocabulary in any language is incredibly extensive, and every country where a same language is spoken has its own set of new words depending on its individual experience, situation and needs. This also applies to different regions within a particular country or continent. For example, in the United Kingdom, the English language in England has differences in terms of vocabulary and accent compared to the one in Scotland, Wales and Northern Ireland. Then, the entire British English is different from the one in Australia, United States and Canada, and so on. Within the USA you can notice changes in pronunciation and words between states, north and south, city and country area, etc.

If we analyze the Spanish language by regions we will find variations too between countries and even within one same country. Through the years, many regional words have been officially accepted and incorporated into the Spanish vocabulary either regionally or internationally; there are always ongoing updates. A good example is "appetizers", which has a long list of Spanish synonyms: "tapas" (Spain), "botanas" (Mexico), "tentempiés" (Argentina), "canapés" (Chile), "pasabocas" (Colombia), and the most international ones "entremeses" and "aperitivos", used regularly in the Caribbean.

Another good example is the word bus = "bus/autobús" (from the French "bus/autobus"), which are the most international ones, and also "guagua" (from Canary Islands, Spain), widely used in the Antilles in their daily standard conversation, along with the less frequently used "autobús". At the same time, in Andean Spanish (Ecuador, Peru, Bolivia, and others in South America), there is a similar native Quechuan word, "wawa", converted to Spanish as "guagua", with a totally different meaning: baby/child.

In the last few decades, there has been an increased English influence on the Spanish language; so many words have been incorporated into the Spanish vocabulary in all countries where Spanish is spoken, not only in a few as some believe, pointing at Mexico for being a neighbor of the USA, and Puerto Rico for being politically related to the USA. But, in reality, even though these are actual reasons, all Spanish-speaking countries (from Spain to anywhere in Latin America) count today with many English words (Anglicisms) incorporated into their local Spanish, due to many other reasons like frequent traveling to and from English speaking countries, international business, e-business, the TV, the Internet, etc. By speaking with people, or reading articles, from any Spanish speaking country, indistinctly, anyone can notice the presence of Anglicisms such as exact words like "test", "cake", "aerobic", "casting", "jeans", "marketing", and "email"; and others that have been adapted, like "parquear" (to park) and "parqueo" (parking lot/spot), "cachar" (to catch), "bife" (beef) and "biftec"/ "bistec" (beef steak) = carne de res; and sport-related ones are very common too, such as "béisbol" (baseball) = "pelota", "básquetbol" (basketball) = "baloncesto", and the very popular "fútbol" (football) = "balompié", including its rules in English.

In the technology world new words are being created constantly, and they either do not have an equivalent in Spanish or it is not practical to find one. Therefore, some of these words have been officially accepted in their original English forms, like Internet and web, and others have been created from English, like scanner = "escáner".

Others existed in Spanish, but a change in their emphasis has been made following the English pronunciation: "coc**tel/cóc**tel", "cho**fer/chó**fer", "vi**deo/ví**deo", etc. [Bold = **Emphasis**]

Now, probably the most relevant case that can be observed these days is "aplicar/aplicación" (to apply/application), which when used in the wrong context becomes the very popular false Anglicism used by a vast number of Spanish speakers in and out of the United States and Canada, present in basically every country where the "Cervantes's language" (Spanish) is spoken. "To Apply" is either "Aplicar" or "Solicitar". These are two different verbs that cannot be exchanged. The same goes with the noun "Application", either "Aplicación" or "Solicitud". "Aplicar" means to apply one thing to another, like paint to a wall, and lotion or cream to the skin; also means to exert something, like force, pressure or knowledge. It cannot replace "solicitar" when **applying for** something. Therefore, to **apply for** a job = "**solicitar** un empleo", not "*aplicar para* un empleo", and the paper form used to apply for that job is "solicitud", not "aplicación". When we apply for ("solicitamos") a job, we apply ("aplicamos") force to the pen, and ink to the application ("solicitud").

INTRODUCTION

Learning a new language is an exciting journey and a very enriching experience. But, it is a challenge that requires time, commitment, and plenty of practice. There are a few things to keep in mind that could help anyone to have a smoother language learning experience.

Languages have rules, but also exceptions to the rules. A good way to approach any new language is by avoiding to think that any given language is the standard, so anything different must be wrong. Also, by keeping in mind not to think in absolute terms; so, thinking of "normally", "usually" or "mostly" instead of "always". Patterns are there and following them is a very helpful learning tool, but many times you will find cases where a pattern (or a rule) does not apply.

Another helpful thing to consider is to observe the similarities between many Spanish and English words. You will find many words that are either identical or similar in spelling. This should not be surprising at all if we look back to both of these languages' origins. They both come from a big family called Indo-European languages, and even though they evolved into two different groups (English is Germanic and Spanish is Italic), Greek, Latin and French (a product of Latin and a sibling of Spanish) played a big role in their formation. Therefore, they both have many prefixes, suffixes, and whole words in common. Additionally, Spanish has been taking many words from English in modern times, this way increasing their similarity.

The Spanish grammar is more complex, compared to English, but its pronunciation is easier because, as opposed to English, a vowel always have the same sound (with just a few exceptions; you were aware this was coming!).

The whole Spanish verb conjugation is divided in four main groups:

	Simple	Compound
Indicative	**Indicative-Simple**	**Indicative-Compound**
Subjunctive	**Subjunctive-Simple**	**Subjunctive-Compound**

One of the reasons why the Spanish grammar is more complex is because of its extensive verb conjugation, which provides more information, such as "who did it" and "how many did it", integrated in the verb. Plus, there are different types of past tenses and moods (indicative and subjunctive) which in English are mostly created by the context within a particular sentence while in Spanish there is a different set of verb conjugation for each case.

Another reason is the fact that nouns, in addition to deal with Number: Singular or Plural, also deal with Gender: Masculine or Feminine; so, everything related to nouns, like articles and adjectives, also need to agree in both gender and number.

Presently, studies show that there are around 350-400 million Spanish speakers around the world (about the same as English). You can add one more to that list: You!

Cardinales / Cardinals

1 = uno
2 = dos
3 = tres
4 = cuatro
5 = cinco
6 = seis
7 = siete
8 = ocho
9 = nueve
10 = diez
11 = once
12 = doce
13 = trece
14 = catorce
15 = quince
16 = dieciséis (diez y seis = ten and six)
17 = diecisiete
18 = dieciocho
19 = diecinueve
20 = veinte
21 = veintiuno (veinte y uno = twenty and one)
/
30 = treinta
31 = treinta y uno (words are written separately)
/
40 = cuarenta
41 = cuarenta y uno
/

50 = cincuenta
60 = sesenta
70 = setenta
80 = ochenta
90 = noventa
100 = cien
101 = ciento uno
/
200 = doscientos
300 = trescientos
400 = cuatrocientos
500 = quinientos
600 = seiscientos
700 = setecientos
800 = ochocientos
900 = novecientos
1.000 = mil
10.000 = diez mil
100.000 = cien mil
1.000.000 = un millón
1.000.000.000 = mil millones (one billion)*
1.000.000.000.000 = un billón (one trillion)*

Note:
Compared to English, the punctuation is reversed for integers and decimals: 1.000 = One thousand (1,000); 0,5 = One half (0.5 = ½).

(*These two are confusing. The tendency is to think: billion = billón)

Ordinales / Ordinals

1st = primero
2nd = segundo
3rd = tercero
4th = cuarto
5th = quinto
6th = sexto
7th = séptimo
8th = octavo
9th = noveno
10th = décimo
11th = décimo primero / undécimo
12th = décimo segundo / duodécimo
13th = décimo tercero
14th = décimo cuarto
/
20th = vigésimo
21st = vigésimo primero
/
30th = trigésimo
40th = cuadragésimo
50th = quincuagésimo
60th = sexagésimo
70th = septuagésimo
80th = octogésimo
90th = nonagésimo
100th = centésimo

As opposed to English, in Spanish, days and months are not written with a capital letter (unless they are at the beginning of a sentence). Plus, the first day of the week is Monday.

Ex:
Hoy es <u>lunes</u>. (Today is <u>Monday</u>)
Hoy es 8 de <u>febrero</u>. (Today is <u>February</u> 8)

Monday = Lunes
Tuesday = Martes
Wednesday = Miércoles
Thursday = Jueves
Friday = Viernes
Saturday = Sábado
Sunday = Domingo

January = Enero
February = Febrero
March = Marzo
April = Abril
May = Mayo
June = Junio
July = Julio
August = Agosto
September = Septiembre
October = Octubre
November = Noviembre
December = Diciembre

Winter = Invierno
Spring = Primavera
Summer = Verano
Fall/Autumn = Otoño

Cold = Frío
Warm = Tibio
Hot = Caliente
Heat = Calor

Wave = Onda
Front = Frente

Rain = Lluvia / To rain = Llover
Rainy = Lluvioso
Snow = Nieve / To snow = Nevar
Snowy = Nevado
Cloud = Nube
Cloudy = Nublado
Wind = Viento
Windy = Ventoso
Thunder = Trueno
Lightning = Relámpago, Rayo

Tropical = Tropical
Depression = Depresión
Storm = Tormenta
Hurricane = Huracán
Tornado/Twister = Tornado

Vocales / Vowels

A (ah)
E (eh)*
I (ee)*
O (oh)
U (oo; as in roof, loop, cook)

(*These two vowels require special attention)

Consonantes / Consonants

H: silent, unless preceded by "c" (as in Chile, chili).
Hoy (Today); Hay (There is/are); Hijo (Son)

J: close to English "H", as in ham, hope, hit.
Jamón (Ham)

Combinations

CC: like "x".
Acción (Action)

LL: close to English "J", as in John, or "G", as in Geography.
Llamar (to call)

C + vowel

Ca: C sounds like "k".
Ce: like "s" (Latin America), English "th" (Spain)
Ci: "s" or "th"
Co: "k"
Cu: "k"

* C has two different sounds:
Hard (like a "k"), when followed by "a", "o" or "u".
Soft, when followed by "e" or "i":
In Spain is like English "th" in "think".
In Latin America, like "s" in "set".

C is the default letter, substituted by Z when needed; when preceding an "a", "o" or "u", but a soft sound is needed:
shoe = zapato ("za" as in "thanks" (Spain): *tha*pato; or as in "Saturday" (Latin America): *sa*pato). If there were a "c" instead of a "z", "<u>c</u>apato", the "c" would have a hard sound like "k", as in "cap" (kap), so it would sound like "*ka*pato". "Z" replaces "C" to make a soft sound in these cases.

Qu + vowel

Qu: "k" sound (silent "u"). Only used followed by "e" or "i".

"<u>Que</u>rer" (As in <u>ke</u>pt) = (to) want, (to) love.

"<u>Qui</u>eres" (As in <u>key</u> or <u>kee</u>p) = You want / You love.

G + vowel

Like English "h" in Her / His	Guttural sound; silent "u"	Guttural sound; "u" is pronounced
[N/A]	Ga → (as in "gamble")	Gua ("guava")
Ge → (as in "her")	Gue → (silent u; "get")	Güe * ("u" is pronounced; "goo-eh")
Gi → (as in "he")	Gui → (silent u; "Guinness")	Güi * ("u" is pronounced; "goo-ey")
[N/A]	Go → ("govern")	Guo ("goo-oh")
[N/A]	Gu ("goo")	[N/A]

* Diéresis (ü): gives "u" its sound (English "oo").

[N/A = Not Applicable]

In Spanish they need two marks: ¿Question? / ¡Exclamation!

Qué = What
Cómo = How
Cuándo = When
Quién/Quiénes = Who (deals with Number)
Dónde = Where
Cuánto/a = How much (not countable; deals with Gender)
Cuántos/as = How many (countable; deals with Gender)
Cuál/Cuáles = Which (which one/ones). Deals with Number.
Por qué = Why

Greetings / Small Talk

Hola, ¿cómo estás? (Hi, how are you?)
- Bien, ¿y tú? (Fine, and you?)

¿Cuál es tu nombre? (Literally: Which one is your name?)
(What is your name?)
- Mi nombre es___. (My name is___)

¿Cómo te llamas? (Literally: How do you call yourself?)
(What is your name?)

- Me llamo_____.
(My name is ___; Literally: I call myself ___)

¡Mucho gusto! / ¡Un placer! (My pleasure!)
- Igualmente. (Likewise / Same here)

¿De dónde eres? (Where are you from?)
- Soy de_____. (I am from ___)

¿Dónde vives? (Where do you live?)
- Vivo en_____.   (I live in _____)

¿A qué te dedicas? / ¿En qué trabajas?
(What do you do for a living?)

Por favor, ¿qué hora es?   (Please, what time is it?)
- Es la una (1:00) / Son las dos (2:00). (It is _____)

¡Gracias! (Thanks!)
- Por nada / A la orden. ("For nothing" / At your service)
(You are welcome)

Compared to English, there are many more articles in Spanish because they include more specific information about the noun: Masculine or Feminine (Gender), Singular or Plural (Number). There has to be a Gender & Number Agreement between the Article and the Noun.

Definite	(the)		Indefinite	(a/an)	(some)
	S	P		S	P
M	el	los		un	unos
F	la	las		una	unas

Neuter: lo (no gender/no number)

SUSTANTIVOS (NOMBRES) / NOUNS

Nouns identify persons and things. They, and anything related to them (articles, adjectives, pronouns), deal with Gender & Number Agreement. The most basic pattern to identify a noun's gender is:

Ending with "o" = Masculine
Ending with "a" = Feminine

But, there are some other ending patterns (with exceptions), like:

Ending with -ma (most, not all) or with a consonant: Masculine
Ending with -ción, -sión, -ad: Feminine

Masculine	Feminine
Libro = Book	Silla = Chair
Cuaderno = Notebook	Pluma = Feather / Pen
Bolígrafo = Pen	Pizarra = White/Black Board
Lápiz = Pencil	Tarea = Task / Homework
Problema = Problem	Asignación = Assignment / Homework
Teorema = Theorem	Universidad = University
Papel = Paper	Presión = Pressure

The **Plural** is formed by adding "s" (if the noun ends with a vowel) or "es" (if the noun ends with a consonant).

Ex:
El libro (The book) : Masculine, Singular
Los libros (The books) : Masculine, Plural
La silla (The chair) : Feminine, Singular
Las sillas (The chairs) : Feminine, Plural
El papel (The paper) : Masculine, Singular
Los papeles (The papers) : Masculine, Plural
La universidad (The university) : Feminine, Singular
Las universidades (The universities) : Feminine, Plural

The **Neuter** (no gender/no number) "**lo**" is used to convert adjectives into nouns as the subject of the sentence (adding "-ness" to adjectives: good → goodness), normally abstract things:

El hombre bueno/El bueno (the good man)

Lo bueno de estudiar español es...

(The goodness about studying Spanish is...)

ADJETIVOS / ADJECTIVES
(Modify nouns)

Descriptivos / Descriptive

Anything that describes or modifies a noun: Colors, Sizes, Shapes, etc. These adjectives, in Spanish, are normally placed after the noun (Noun-Adj.), instead of before, as in English (Adj.-Noun).
There is Gender & Number Agreement.

Examples:
La casa roja (The red house)
El carro blanco (The white car)

Demostrativos / Demonstrative

In English, even though we can refer to three different locations (here = aquí, there = allí, over there = allá), the Demonstrative Adjectives refer to only two different locations, either This/These or That/Those.

In Spanish, each one of the 3 locations (aquí, allí, allá) has a corresponding Dem. Adj. (Again, they deal with number and gender).

Location	Singular	Plural
(Aquí = Here)	Este/Esta = This	Estos/Estas = These
(Allí = There)	Ese/Esa = That	Esos/Esas = Those
(Allá = Over there)	Aquél/Aquella = That	Aquellos/Aquellas = Those

Examples:

Este carro (This car).

Esa calle (That street).

Aquel árbol
(That tree – over there).

Estos carros (These cars).

Esas calles (Those streets).

Aquellos árboles
(Those trees – over there).

Posesivos / Possessive

In Spanish, there has to be an agreement between the Possessive
Adjective and the noun in terms of number only (not gender) with the
exception of Nosotros and Vosotros, which also deal with the gender.

Person	Singular	Plural
1	Mi, Mis = My	Nuestro/a, Nuestros/as = Our
2	Tu, Tus = Your	Vuestro/a, Vuestros/as (Spain) = Your
	Su, Sus = Your	Su, Sus = Your
3	Su, Sus = His/Her	Su, Sus = Their

Mi casa es tu/su casa (My house is your house).
Bienvenido a nuestro hogar (Welcome to our home).
Mis libros y tus libros son nuevos
(My books and your books are new).
Nuestros libros son nuevos (Our books are new).

En Expresiones Comparativas / In Comparative Expressions

Más + **Adj**. + Que = More + **Adj**. + Than (or Adj. + "er" + Than)
Menos + **Adj**. + Que = Less + **Adj**. + Than
Tan + **Adj**. + Como = As + **Adj**. + As

Más caro que / More expensive than

Más barato que / Cheaper than

Menos difícil que / Less difficult than

Tan alto como / As tall as

Ex: Este reloj es más caro que ese reloj.
(This clock/watch is more expensive than that clock/watch).

Expresiones Superlativas / Superlative Expressions

These ones use a definite article: el, la, los, las (the).

El/La/Los/Las más/menos + Adj. =
The most/least + Adj (or Adj. + "est")

El más valioso / The most valuable.

La menos interesante / The least interesting.

Los más altos / The tallest.

There are irregular superlatives:

El (La) mejor   / The best
Los (Las) mejores

El (La) peor   / The worst
Los (Las) peores

Pronouns substitute nouns to avoid repetition, to specify/clarify a subject, or to simplify sentences. Because they are related to nouns, there is a Gender & Number agreement. There are different types in the family:

Demonstrative
Possessive
Subject
Object
Reflexive

Demonstrative Pronouns
(See: Demonstrative Adjectives)

[Accent mark needed only when avoiding ambiguity]
(See: Essential Accented Words)

Location	**Singular**	**Plural**
(Aquí = Here)	Este/a = This one	Estos/as = These ones
(Allí = There)	Ese/a = That one	Esos/as = Those ones
(Allá = Over there)	Aquel/Aquella = That one	Aquellos/as = Those ones

*Neutral Form: Esto, Eso, Aquello

These are the same demonstrative adjectives, but when the noun is not present (removed to avoid repetition), the adjective becomes a pronoun (because now it represents the noun):

Este carro es rojo y ese carro es azul.
(This car is red and that car is blue)

The noun "car" is present. "Este" and "Ese" are adjectives.

If we remove the noun "car":
Este es rojo y ese es azul. (This one is red and that one is blue)

*The **Neutral Form** is used when something has not been defined:

¿Qué es <u>eso</u>? (What is that?)
- <u>Eso</u> es una casa. (That is a house)

Now, after knowing what it is, we know the G & N, so we can state its name with its corresponding adjective:

<u>Esa</u> casa es blanca. (That house is white)

Pronombres Posesivos / Possessive Pronouns
(See: Possessive Adjectives)

Mío/a/os/as = Mine	Nuestro/a/os/as = Ours
Tuyo/a/os/as = Yours	Vuestro/a/os/as = Yours
Suyo/a/os/as	Suyo/a/os/as
Suyo/a/os/as = His/Hers	Suyo/a/os/as = Theirs

When using a possessive adjective, if the noun is not present (removed to avoid repetition), the adjective becomes a pronoun (because now it represents the noun):

Mi carro es rojo y tu carro es azul.
(My car is red and your car is blue)

The Noun "car" is present. "Mi" and "Tu" are adjectives.

If we remove the noun "car":

El mío es rojo y el tuyo es azul.
(Mine is red and yours is blue)

(or with the noun present, as adjectives, when placed after the noun, as opposed to before the noun (tu carro = el carro tuyo):

El carro mío (mi carro) es rojo y el carro tuyo (tu carro) es azul]

¿De quién es este carro?
(Whose car is this?)

- Es mío. / Este carro es mío.
(It is mine) / (This car is mine)

Person	Singular	Plural
1	**Yo = I**	**Nosotros/as = We**
2	**Tú = You** (informal) →	**Vosotros/as = You** (Spain)
	Usted = You (formal) →	**Ustedes = You** (Latin America)
3	**Él/Ella = He/She**	**Ellos/Ellas = They**

Vosotros: Plural of Tú. (Spain)
Ustedes: Plural of Tú and Usted. (Latin America)

VERBOS / VERBS
(express actions)

Spanish does not have an auxiliary verb (like "do / does") to form questions and negatives. "No" alone is placed before the verb.
As opposed to English, Spanish does have double negative.

Verbs are divided in 2 parts: Stem + Ending

Verb Endings in infinitive: ar, er, ir

A verb in infinitive means that it has not been conjugated (adapted to 1st, 2nd or 3rd person, singular or plural); like "to" + verb.

(to) study = estudiar: estudi - ar
                              (stem) - (ending)

Verb Conjugation

Compared to English, verb conjugation in Spanish is a lot more complicated because the "endings" give more information about the "action", like the Person (who did it), and the Number (how many did it).

The ar, er, ir endings are replaced by new ones, according to the Person (1st, 2nd, 3rd) and the Number (Singular or Plural).

The 2nd person singular (Usted) and the 3rd person (Él/Ella) have the same ending.

The 2nd person plural (Ustedes) and the 3rd person plural (Ellos/as) have the same ending.

-ar (the regular pattern is: o, as, a, amos, áis, an)

Person	Singular	Plural
1	Yo Stem + o	Nosotros/as Stem + amos
2	Tú + as →	Vosotros/as + áis
	Usted + a →	Ustedes + **an**
3	Él/Ella + **a**	Ellos/as + **an**

Hablar (to speak/to talk)

Person	Singular	Plural
1	Yo hablo	Nosotros/as hablamos
2	Tú hablas	Vosotros/as habláis
	Usted habl**a**	Ustedes habl**an**
3	Él/Ella habl**a**	Ellos/as habl**an**

Negative: Yo **no** hablo francés (I **do not** speak French)

-er (the regular pattern is: o, es, e, ̱emos, éis, en)

Leer (to read)

Person	Singular	Plural
1	Yo leo	Nosotros/as leemos
2	Tú lees	Vosotros/as leéis
	Usted le**e**	Ustedes le**en**
3	Él/Ella le**e**	Ellos/as le**en**

Negative: Yo **no leo**, Tú **no lees**, etc.

-ir (the regular pattern is: o, es, e, imos, ís, en)

Escribir (to write)

Person	Singular	Plural
1	Yo escribo	Nosotros/as escribimos
2	Tú escribes	Vosotros/as escribís
	Usted escribe	Ustedes escrib**en**
3	Él/Ella escrib**e**	Ellos/as escrib**en**

Negative: Yo **no escribo,** Tú **no escribes,** etc.

Double Negative:

Ellos **no** hacen **nada** / They **do not** do **anything**
(Literally: They **do not** do **nothing**)

Tú **no** lees **ningún** libro / You **do not** read **any** book
(Lit.: You **do not** read **no** book)

No llames **nunca** / **Do not ever** call
(Lit.: **Do not never** call)

No vemos a **nadie** aquí / We **do not** see **anybody** here
(Lit.: We **do not** see **nobody** here)

Stem Changes

As explained in the Verbs section, verbs are divided in Stem and Ending. In Stem-changing verbs, the vowel preceding the infinitive verb ending (ar, er, ir) changes when conjugated in the Present Indicative tense, **except** for 1st person plural (nosotros) and 2nd person plural (vosotros). There are many verbs in this family. The **most common** stem changes are: **e to i, e to ie, and o to ue**. Rare to find are: i to ie, and u to ue. Some examples:

Keep the **Conjugation Table** and the **L** shape in mind:

Subject Pronouns:

Yo	Nosotros/as
Tú	Vosotros/as
Usted	Ustedes
Ellos/as	Ellos/as

e → i

Pedir (to ask for, to order)

Pido	Pedimos
Pides	Pedís
Pide	Piden
Pide	Piden

Medir (To measure): Mido, Mides, Mide, Medimos, etc.

e → ie

Qu**e**rer (to want / to love)

Quiero	Queremos
Quieres	Queréis
Quiere	Quieren
Quiere	Quieren

Sentir (To feel): Siento, Sientes, Siente, Sentimos, etc.

o → ue

P**o**der (to be able: "can")

Puedo	Podemos
Puedes	Podéis
Puede	Pueden
Puede	Pueden

Mover (To move): Muevo, Mueves, Mueve, Movemos, etc.

i → ie

Adqu**i**rir (to acquire)

Adquiero	Adquirimos
Adquieres	Adquirís
Adquiere	Adquieren
Adquiere	Adquieren

u → ue

J**u**gar (to play)

Juego	Jugamos
Juegas	Jugáis
Juega	Juegan
Juega	Juegan

Consonant changes (Special Consonant-Vowel pairs)
(See: Pronunciation)

These verb families, in their Present Indicative tense, deal with changing certain consonants before vowels in order to keep the original sound from their infinitive form. There are many within each family.

g → j (in the "yo" form)

1. Proteger (to protect):
protejo, proteges, protege, protegemos, protegéis, protegen

2. Escoger (to choose)

c → z (in the "yo" form)

1. Convencer (to convince):
convenzo, convences, convence, convencemos, convencéis, convencen

2. Vencer (to defeat, win)

gu → g (in the "yo" form)

1. Distinguir (to distinguish):
distingo, distingues, distingue, distinguimos, distinguís, distinguen

2. Extinguir (to extinguish)

Other Changes

These verb families, in their Present Indicative tense, involve irregular spelling but following a pattern; there are many of them within each group.

"yo-g" (added "g" in the "yo" form only)

1. Poner (to put): pongo, pones, pone, ponemos, ponéis, ponen

2. Tener (to have)

"yo-z" (added "z" in the "yo" form only)

1. Conducir (to conduct, to drive):
conduzco, conduces, conduce, conducimos, conducís, conducen

2. Producir (to produce)

"yo-ig" (added "ig" in the "yo" form only)

1. Traer (to bring): traigo, traes, trae, traemos, traéis, traen

2. Caer (to fall)

"added y" (except in "nosotros" and "vosotros")

1. Contribuir (to contribute):
contribuyo, contribuyes, contribuye, contribuimos, contribuís, contribuyen

2. Construir (to build, to construct)

*A = to, at
Ante = before (in front, facing)
Bajo = under
Con = with
Contra = against
*De = of, from, about
Desde = from, since
Durante = during
En = in, at
Entre = between, among
Hacia = toward
Hasta = until
Mediante = by means of, by
*Para = for, to, in order to
*Por = for, by, through, during, per
Según = according to
Sin = without
Sobre = on, over, above, about
Tras = after

(*explained in detail ahead)

Pronouns after Prepositions
(except: bajo, entre, según)

Subject (Personal) Pronouns:
yo, tú, usted, él/ella, nosotros/as, vosotros/as, ustedes, ellos/as.

But, **after Prepositions:**
mí, ti, usted, él/ella, nosotros/as, vosotros/as, ustedes, ellos/as.
(exception: con → con**mi**go, con**ti**go)

Prepositions "a" and "de" combined with the singular-masculine definite article "el" only, become one word. (See: Articles)

a + el → al / de + el → del

Ver a (el niño / la niña) / To see (the boy / the girl)
Veo al niño. (I see the boy) / Veo a la niña. (I see the girl)

When combining "a" or "de" with the rest of the articles, they are written separately: al (a el), a la, a los, a las; del (de el), de la, de los, de las.

Preposition "a"

[a = to, at; and other uses]

This preposition is a single letter but there is a lot to say about it.

1. Used when expressing displacement (movement with direction) TO a destination: Ir a (to go to), Venir a (to come to), Llegar a (to arrive to), Regresar/Volver a (to return to, to come back to), etc.
The applicable common question is: "Where (to)?"

Manu va a la universidad. (Manu goes to the university)

2. Personal "a". Used when the recipient (Direct Object = Objeto/Complemento Directo; Acusativo) of the action is a person. (See: Direct Objects)

[*Conocer = to Know] (*See: Verbs with Spelling Changes)

Conozco el libro de español. (I know the Spanish book)
Conozco a Manu. (I know Manu)

3. To express values like distance, speed, price, time (of an event, NOT the present time).

La ciudad está a 1 hora de aquí. (The city is 1 hour away from here)
La ciudad está a 60 kilómetros de aquí.
(The city is 60 kms away from here)

El avión viaja a 600 km/hr. (The airplane travels at 600 km/hr)

El salmón está a $4/lb hoy. (Salmon is at $4/lb today)

La clase de español es a las 9:00 AM.
(The Spanish class is at 9:00 AM)

4. Used in some expressions related to human senses, taking the place of "like" to express similarity.

Huele a pizza. (Smells like pizza)   [Oler = to smell]
Suena a carro viejo. (Sounds like an old car)   [Sonar = to sound]
Sabe a pollo. (Tastes like chicken)
[Saber = to taste (by itself); NOT "to taste something (saborear)";
NOT "to Know (saber/conocer)"].

Preposition "de"

[de = of, from; and other uses]

1. Used to express displacement (movement with direction) like "a" but in the opposite direction, FROM an origin: Ir de ... a... (To go from ... to ...), Venir de (to come from), Llegar de (to arrive from), Regresar/Volver de (to return from / to come back from), etc.
The applicable common question is: "Where (from)?"

Nydia viene de la escuela. (Nydia comes from school)

2. To state the material of which something is made (made of ...).

La camisa de algodón. (The cotton shirt)
Es de algodón. / Está hecha de algodón. (It is made of cotton)

3. To express possession ('s).

El libro de Nydia. (Nydia's book)

4. To state the topic being discussed.

El libro es de* español (The book is about Spanish)
(*Also: "acerca de", "sobre")

5. Combined with "a", expresses the start and end (parameters) of distances, speeds, prices, times, and others.

El efecto dura de 20 a 24 hrs.
(approximation: The effect lasts from 20 to 24 hrs.)

La clase es de 9:00 AM a 11:00 AM.
(The class is from 9:00 AM to 11:00 AM)

Los precios son de $10 a $20. (The prices are from $10 to $20)

El carro acelera de 0 a 60 kph en 5 segundos.
(The car accelerates from 0 to 60 kph in 5 seconds)

Prepositions "Para" and "Por"

Use "para" when expressing:

Purpose:

¿Para qué es un lápiz? (What is a pencil for?)
- Para escribir.   (For writing)

Comparison:

Para ser tu segundo idioma, ya sabes mucho.
(For being your second language, you already know a lot)

Deadline:

La tarea es para mañana. (The homework is for tomorrow)

Destination / Recipient:

Voy para Canadá hoy. (I am going to Canada today)

El libro es para ti. (The book is for you)

Use "por" when expressing:

Exchange:

Pagaste $20 por la camisa. (You paid $20 for the shirt)

Replacement:

Voy a trabajar por ti mañana porque estás enfermo.
(I am going to work for you tomorrow because you are sick)

Moving through / throughout:

Pasando por la puerta. (Passing through the door)
Paseando por el centro de la ciudad. (Strolling throughout downtown)

Duration:

Pam estudió por 3 horas. (Pam studied for 3 hours)

Means of transportation:

Voy por avión. (I go by airplane)

Reason:

Obtuviste una F por no estudiar. (You got an F for not studying)

Units of Measurements:

70 millas por hora. (70 miles per hour)

HACER
(To Do & To Make)

"Hacer" is a verb with multiple uses and has two meanings in English: To Do and To Make.

Hacer la tarea. (To do the homework)
Hacer un edificio. (To make a building)

(See: Verbs with Spelling Changes: "yo-g")

Person	S	P
1	Hago	Hacemos
2	Haces	Hacéis
	Hace	Hacen
3	Hace	Hacen

Hace

In this form, "hace", it has different uses.

To express weather conditions:

Hace calor. (It is hot)
Hace frío. (It is cold)
Hace viento. (It is windy)

To express elapsed time:

It could be used as "ago" for something that happened once:

Hace 10 años (que) estudié francés. (I studied French 10 years ago)
(note verb "estudiar" in past tense)

Combined with "que" (Hace + Time period + que) and the verb in present tense refers to something that started in the past and continues as of today:

Hace 2 semanas que estudio francés.
(It has been 2 weeks studying French)

Or (Desde hace + Time period):

Estudio francés desde hace 2 semanas.
(I have been studying French since 2 weeks ago)

(note verb "estudiar" in present tense)

TENER
(To have)

There are many things to mention about this verb, in terms of spelling, meaning and use.

First, "tener" has two different spelling changes combined: "yo-g" and e→ie. (See: Spelling Changes):

Tener (To have)

Person	S	P
1	Tengo	Tenemos
2	Tienes	Tenéis
	Tiene	Tienen
3	Tiene	Tienen

It is also irregular in its past and future tenses
(See: Preterit & Future).

In addition to its normal use comparable to the English "to have = to possess", "tener" expresses a variety of personal states or conditions, not comparable to the English counterparts (where the verb "to be" is used instead):

Tengo hambre. ("I have hunger") = I am hungry.
Tienes sed. ("You have thirst") = You are thirsty.
Tiene frío. ("He/She has coldness") = He/She is cold.
Tenemos calor. ("We have heat") = We are hot.
Tenéis sueño. ("You have sleepiness") = You (plural) are sleepy.
Tienen 30 años. ("They have 30 years") = They are 30 years old.

Tener que...
Also, when "tener" is combined with "que" expresses obligation;
Tener que... = To have to...

Tienes que leer más. = You have to read more.

Main Verb: ¿Hay o no hay?

"Haber" is a Main and an Auxiliary Verb. As a main verb is used to express the existence/presence of things or people, **"hay"**, for both singular and plural forms. Also to express obligation, **"hay + que"**.

Hay = There is
       There are

Hay un libro. (There is a book / There is one book)
Hay dos libros. (There are two books)
Hay libros. (There are books)
Ex: Hay libros en la biblioteca. (There are books in the library)

Hay una persona. (There is a person, there is one person)
Hay dos personas. (There are two persons)
Hay personas. (There are persons)
Ex: Hay personas en la casa. (There are persons in the house)

¿Hay alguien en casa? (Is there anyone home?)

¿Hay pan? (Is there any bread?)
- No, no hay. (No, there is not)
Debería haber pan. (There should be bread)
Tiene que haber pan. (There has to be bread)

Hay que...

Combined with "que" expresses obligation (impersonal):

"Hay que" comprar pan. ("It is necessary" to buy bread).

[Note that it does not specify who has to buy it (impersonal)]

Auxiliary Verb

"Haber" is also used as an auxiliary verb to form compound tenses, like in English when "have" is used as an auxiliary verb for the same purpose.
(See: Compound Tenses)

SER y ESTAR
(To Be)

"To be" is a very important verb in both English and Spanish. It means either **"Ser"** or **"Estar"**; therefore it requires some further analysis in order to know which one you should choose.

Person	Ser		Estar	
	S	P	S	P
1	Soy	Somos	Estoy	Estamos
2	Eres	Sois	Estás	Estáis
	Es	Son	Está	Están
3	Es	Son	Está	Están

Ser

One of its main characteristics is to refer to permanent things. But use "Ser" when expressing:

Origin & Nationality
¿De dónde eres? (Where are you from?)
- Soy de Italia / Soy italiano*. (I am from Italy) / (I am Italian)

Physical attribute / Personality
Manu es alto. / Nydia es amable. (Manu is tall) / (Nydia is kind)

Possession
Esa es mi casa. (That is my house)

Profession
Cano es contable. (Cano is an accountant)

Date & Time
El concierto es el 5 de marzo*. (The concert is on March the 5th)
¿Qué hora es? (What time is it?)

Information about an event (including location)
El juego de baloncesto es en Miami y es a las 6 PM.
(The basketball game is in Miami and it is at 6 PM)

*In Spanish, nationalities, months and days do not start with a capital letter.

Estar

One of its main characteristics is to refer to temporary things.
But use "Estar" when expressing:

Mood
Pam está contenta. (Pam is happy)

Physical condition
Tito está enfermo. (Tito is sick)

Result of an action
Sofy está sentada / parada. (Sofy is sitting down / standing up)

Location
Ellos están en la playa. (They are at the beach)

Contrasting Ser and Estar:

Juana está en la escuela. Ella es maestra.
(Juana is in school. She is a teacher.)

Yo soy de Alaska, pero estoy en Canadá.
(I am from Alaska, but I am in Canada)

El café es bueno, pero este café está malo.
(Coffee is good, but this coffee is bad)

Jonás es músico. Él está en una banda musical.
(Jonás is a musician. He is in a musical band.)

Él es listo* y está listo* para el examen.
(He is smart and he is ready for the test)

Joe es fotógrafo, pero está en mercadeo ahora.
(Joe is a photographer, but he is in marketing now)

Jonás y Joe son primos. Ahora están en el parque.
(Jonás and Joe are cousins. Now they are in the park.)

Iván es mi hermano y está en Francia, pero es de España.
(Iván is my brother and he is in France, but he is from Spain)

* "Listo" and other verbs change their meaning by using Ser or Estar.

SABER y CONOCER
(To Know)

To Know is another very important verb in English as well as in Spanish and, like To Be, also has two equivalents: **"Saber"** and **"Conocer"**.

	Saber		Conocer	
Person	S	P	S	P
1	Sé	Sabemos	Conozco	Conocemos
2	Sabes	Sabéis	Conoces	Conocéis
	Sabe	Saben	Conoce	Conocen
3	Sabe	Saben	Conoce	Conocen

Use "saber" when you know:

Information
¿Sabes a qué hora es el juego?
(Do you know at what time is the game?)
- Sí, yo sé. Es a las 2:00 PM. (Yes, I know. It is at 2:00 PM).

A topic
¿Sabes francés? (Do you know French?)
- No, no sé francés. Yo sé español.
(No, I do not know French. I know Spanish.)

How to do things
Yo sé llegar al restaurante. (I know how to get to the restaurant).
Tú sabes hablar español. (You know how to speak Spanish).

Use "conocer" when you know:

People
Yo conozco a* Julia. (I know Julia)

(*Personal "a". See Prepositions.)

Places (No "personal a")
¿Conoces un buen restaurante? (Do you know a good restaurant?)
- Sí, conozco un buen restaurante en el centro de la ciudad.
(Yes, I know a good restaurant in downtown.)

Yo conozco las Cataratas del Niágara. (I know Niagara Falls)

Works (movies, plays, books, buildings, art, music)
¿Conoces una buena película de acción?
(Do you know a good action movie?)

Julia conoce el libro de español. (Julia knows the Spanish book)

Ella conoce las pinturas famosas.
(She knows the famous paintings)

Contrasting Saber and Conocer:

Tú conoces a Iván y sabes dónde vive.
(You know Iván and you know where he lives)

Ellos conocen el libro y saben que es de español.
(They know the book and know that it is about Spanish)

Ustedes conocen al autor y saben de qué es el libro.
(You know the author and know what the book is about)

Yo sé que es una película de ficción, pero no conozco a los actores.
(I know that it is a fiction movie, but I do not know the actors)

¿Quién conoce la canción?
(Who knows the song?)

¿Quién sabe de quién es?
(Who knows whose is it?)

Adverbs do to verbs what adjectives do to nouns. They modify or add information. Noun-Adjective / Verb-Adverb.

To describe how something is done
Basically, take an adjective and add the ending –mente (like in English: -ly) to create an adverb, which will accompany a verb.
Cuidadoso/a = Careful (adj); Cuidadosamente = Carefully (adv).
(for Masculine adjectives, change the "o" at the end to "a", and add -mente)

La niña cuidadosa (the careful girl)
    n.   adj.

La niña camina cuidadosamente (the girl walks carefully)
        v.   adv.

El niño cuidadoso / El niño camina cuidadosamente

To describe where something/someone is (LOCATION)
Adverbs also tell the location of people/things with respect to other people/things. Add the preposition "de". (NOTE: de + el → del)

Encima (on top of, over, on)
Debajo (under, below, underneath)
Al lado (beside, next to)
Enfrente (across from)   +   "de"
Detrás (behind)
Dentro (in)
Fuera (out)
Alrededor (around)

Notice the verb "estar" (one of its main uses is to express location) and the information about location that follows it.

El gato <u>está</u> <u>encima</u> del carro. (The cat is on the car)
         v.   adv.

El gato <u>está</u> <u>debajo</u> del carro. (The cat is under the car)

El gato <u>está</u> <u>dentro</u> del carro. (The cat is in the car)

Also to express these locations:
"Aquí" (here), "Allí" / "Ahí" (there), "Allá" (over there).

These are related to the Demonstrative Adjectives/Pronouns "este", "ese", "aquel", etc. (See: Adjectives & Pronouns).

Los libros están aquí. (The books are here)

Antes de
Después de
*Tener que
*Hay que
*Deber   +   V (infinitive)
*Deber de
*Necesitar
*Querer
*Ir a
*Empezar/Comenzar a
*Acabar/Terminar de
*Soler/Acostumbrar

Antes = Before

                                +   de   +   Verb in Infinitive (ar, er, ir)
Después = After

<u>Después de salir</u> de la casa, tú siempre cierras la puerta.
(<u>After leaving</u> the house, you always close the door)

*Double Verbs

As a general rule, the first verb is conjugated (in any tense) and the second one remains in infinitive.

Tener que = to have an obligation (someone "has to" do something)

Ustedes <u>tienen que hacer</u> su tarea. (You <u>have to do</u> your homework)

<u>Tenemos que comprar</u> pan. (We <u>have to buy</u> bread)

Hay que = there is an obligation
(something "has to be done"; impersonal)
"Hay" comes from the main verb "haber", which only conjugates in 3rd
person singular, in any tense.
(See: Haber)

Hay que comprar pan. (It is necessary to buy bread)
(Impersonal. It does not specify who has to buy it)

Deber = Must / Should. (Duty / Suggestion (See: Conditional Tense))

Ustedes deben comprar el libro. (You must buy (duty) the book)

Tú deberías dormir mejor. (You should sleep (suggestion) better)

Deber (de) = Probability.

Debe (de) ser como la 1:00 ya.
(It should/must be around 1:00 already)

Necesitar = (to) need

Nosotros necesitamos estudiar más. (We need to study more)

Querer = (to) want
(also means "to love"; not used in this structure)

Yo quiero aprender italiano. (I want to learn Italian)

Ir a = (to) go to

Normalmente, voy a correr a las 7:00 PM.
(Normally, I go to run at 7:00 PM)

Also, to refer to the future using a present tense
(like "going to" + verb):

Voy a trabajar mañana. / I am going to work tomorrow.
(Present Indicative)   (Present Progressive)

Tú vas a viajar este lunes. (You are going to travel this Monday)

Empezar/Comenzar a = (to) start/begin doing something.

Empiezas/Comienzas a estudiar a las 6:00.
(You start studying at 6:00)

Acabar/Terminar de = (to) end/finish doing something.

Acabas*/Terminas de estudiar a las 8:00. (You finish studying at 8:00)

*Also:
Acabas de leer esta oración. (You just finished reading this sentence)
(Pres.)

Soler/Acostumbrar = (to) do something regularly. Usually.

Suelo/Acostumbro asistir de noche. (I usually attend at night)

This form expresses an action (in any tense) happening during a length of time, which when used in its present tense refers to "as we speak". It is formed by dropping the verb ending and replacing it with –ando or –iendo.

ar → ando
er / ir → iendo

Hablar → Hablando
Comer → Comiendo
Subir → Subiendo

As in English, this tense normally appears accompanied by another verb:
To be. In Spanish, to be = Ser or Estar, being **"estar"** the one used here, **conjugated in any tense** and followed by a second verb in "ing" form.

Estar

Person	S	P
1	Estoy	Estamos
2	Estás	Estáis
	Está	Están
3	Está	Están

Estar + V (ing)

Estoy escribiendo acerca del gerundio.
(I am writing about the gerund)

Tú estás estudiando este tema. (You are studying this topic)

Andar (to go or be around) and **Seguir** (to keep or continue) are also commonly used combined with the gerund, like "estar":

Él anda comprando algo. (He is around buying something)

Yo sigo escribiendo acerca del gerundio.
(I keep writing about the gerund)

It is not used as a subject, like English does; Spanish uses an infinitive:

Running is good for your health. /
(Gerund)

(El) Correr es bueno para tu salud.
   (Infinitive)

PRONOMBRES DE COMPLEMENTO (OBJETO) / OBJECT PRONOUNS

Pronouns replace nouns (persons or things) to avoid repetition. Object Pronouns (OPs) specify who/what is directly affected by the action done (verb): **Direct Object**, and who/what is the recipient (to whom): **Indirect Object**. (Gender & Number Agreement in some cases)

1. When the verb is **Conjugated**, the OP is placed before the verb.

2. When the verb is in **Infinitive** (in a 2-verb structure), the OP is (a) placed before the conjugated verb, or (b) attached to the end of the infinitive.
(See: Additional Sentence Structures)

3. When the verb is in **Gerund** (in a 2-verb structure), the OP is (a) placed before the conjugated verb, or (b) attached to the end of the gerund.
(See: Present Progressive / Gerund)

Pronombres de Complemento (Objeto) Directo: Acusativo / Direct Object Pronouns (DOP)

Person	S	P
1	me	nos
2	te (tú)	os (vosotros)
	lo/la* (usted)	los/las* (ustedes)
3	lo/la*	los/las*

*Remember the basic endings: Masculine "o" and Feminine "a".

Note:
If the Direct Objects are persons (or pets), they appear preceded by an "a" (See: Prepositions / "Personal a"), not to be confused with the "a" always preceding the Indirect Objects.

The direct object (DO) is found right after the verb or responding to the question "what?" or "who?" See the three cases:

[Bread = Pan (**3rd person, masculine, singular**): "**el** pan".
To buy = Comprar]

1. When the verb is Conjugated:

Yo <u>compro</u> <u>pan</u>. (I <u>buy</u> <u>bread</u>)
   Verb   DO   V   DO

I buy (what?) bread. Bread is the DO, so its DOP is "**lo**".

Yo <u>lo</u> <u>compro</u>. (I buy <u>it</u>)
 DOP   V

2. When the verb is in Infinitive (Ir a + Infinitive):

<u>Voy a comprar</u> <u>pan</u>. (<u>I am going to buy</u> <u>bread</u>)
     V   DOP

(a) <u>Lo</u> voy a comprar.

(b) Voy a comprar<u>lo</u>. (I am going to buy <u>it</u>)

3. When the verb is in Gerund:

<u>Estoy comprando</u> <u>pan</u>. (I <u>am buying</u> <u>bread</u>)

(a) <u>Lo</u> estoy comprando.

(b) Estoy comprándo<u>lo</u>. (I am buying <u>it</u>)

If the DO is a person (or a pet) it is preceded by a "personal a":
Yo veo <u>a Salma</u>. (I see Salma) → Yo <u>la</u> veo.
Voy a ver <u>a Salma</u> → <u>La</u> voy a ver. / Voy a ver<u>la</u>.
Estoy viendo <u>a Salma</u> → <u>La</u> estoy viendo. / Estoy viéndo<u>la</u>.

Pronombres de Complemento (Objeto) Indirecto: Dativo / Indirect Object Pronouns (IOP)

Person	S	P
1	me	nos
2	te (tú)	os (vos.)
	le (ud.)	les (uds.)
3	le	les

The indirect object (IO), the recipient, is found right after the preposition "a", or responding to the question "to whom?". The most common way is having the IOP in the sentence, either with the IO included (redundant*) or without it. See the three cases:

[café = coffee]

1. Conjugated

Tú das café a Nadia. (You give coffee to (whom?) Nadia)
   V   DO   IO   V   DO   IO (3rd, S)

Tú le das café (*a Nadia). (You give her coffee)
   IOP V

2. Infinitive

Vas a dar café a Nadia. (You are going to give coffee to Nadia)

"Vas a dar" comes from the 2-verb structure Ir a + V (infinitive), where the first verb "Ir" is conjugated in any tense and the second verb remains in infinitive. Take the entire "vas a dar" as The Verb, therefore place the OP before it (separately) or after it (together).
(See: Additional Sentence Structures)

(a) Le vas a dar café (*a Nadia). (You are going to give her coffee)

(b) Vas a darle café (*a Nadia).

3. Gerund

<u>Estás dando</u> café a <u>Nadia</u>. (You are giving coffee to Nadia)

"Estás dando" comes from the 2-verb structure Estar + V (gerund: "ing"), where the first verb "Estar" is conjugated in any tense and the second verb is in gerund. Take the entire "estás dando" as The Verb, and place the OP before it (separately) or after it (together).
(See: Present Progressive / Gerund)

(a) <u>Le</u> estás dando café (*a Nadia).   (You are giving <u>her</u> coffee)

(b) Estás dándo<u>le</u> café (*a Nadia).

Doble Pronombre / Double Object Pronoun (2OP)

Both Objects (Direct and Indirect) can be replaced by their corresponding Pronouns and put together, Double Object Pronoun (2OP), in the same sentence, but reversed: IOP-DOP. When using 2OP, the **Indirect Object Pronouns (IOP)** **le** and **les** become **se** (singular and plural).

Direct Object Pronouns (DOP)

Person	S	P
1	me	nos
2	te	os
	lo/la	los/las
3	lo/la	los/las

Indirect Object Pronouns (IOP) / **When using 2OP**

Person	S	P		S	P
1	me	nos		me	nos
2	te	os		te	os
	le	**les**	→	**se**	**se**
3	**le**	**les**	→	**se**	**se**

The three cases seen for DOP and IOP apply to 2OP:

1. When the verb is Conjugated, the 2OP are placed before the verb and in **reversed order**, so the original order V, DO, IO is reversed: IO, DO, V.

Ex 1: [traer = to bring; café = coffee; su tío = her uncle]

Noelia <u>trae</u> <u>café</u> a <u>su tío</u>. (Noelia brings coffee to her uncle)
      V   DO   IO

Order in sentence → Verb **(1)**, DO **(2)**, IO **(3)**:

Review

Using DOP

Noelia lo trae a su tío. (Noelia brings it to her uncle)

Using IOP

Noelia **le** trae café. (Noelia brings him coffee)

Using 2OP → IOP (3), DOP (2), Verb (1):

Noelia **se**   lo   trae.   (Noelia brings it to him)
      IOP   DOP   Verb

["le" becomes "se"]

Ex 2:

[traer = to bring; comida = food; sus amigas = his friends)

Fran trae comida a sus amigas.
    1   2 (la)   3 **(les)**

(Fran brings food to his friends)

Review

DOP

Fran la trae a sus amigas. (Fran brings it to his friends)

IOP

Fran **les** trae comida. (Fran brings them food)

2OP

Fran **se** la trae. (Fran brings it to them) / ["les" becomes "se"]
   3 2 1

2. When the verb is in Infinitive (in a 2-verb structure: the 1st one is conjugated, the 2nd one is in infinitive), the 2OP are (a) placed before the conjugated verb and in **reversed order**, so the original V, DO, IO is reversed: IO, DO, V, or (b) attached to the end of the Infinitive and also reversed: IO-DO. (See: Additional Sentence Structures)

[ofrecer = to offer]

Tú <u>vas a ofrecer</u> <u>café</u> a <u>Noelia</u>.
      1 (V)   2 (lo)   3 (**le**)

(a) Tú **<u>se</u>** <u>lo</u> <u>vas a ofrecer</u>.   ("le" becomes "se")
     3 2   1

(b) Tú vas a ofrecér<u>selo</u>.

3. When the verb is in Gerund (in a 2-verb structure: the 1st one is conjugated, the 2nd one is in gerund), the 2OP are (a) placed before the conjugated verb and in **reversed order**, so the original V, DO, IO is reversed: IO, DO, V, or (b) attached to the end of the Gerund and also reversed: IO-DO. (See: Present Progressive / Gerund)

Tú <u>estás ofreciendo</u> <u>café</u> a <u>Fran</u>.
          1   2   3

(a) Tú <u>se</u> <u>lo</u> <u>estás ofreciendo</u>.
     3 2 1

(b) Tú estás ofreciéndo<u>selo</u>.

Note: Normally, the IOP is in the sentence, either with the IO (redundantly) or without it (as seen in the IOP section): (1) Noelia se lo trae (a su tío), Fran se la trae (a sus amigas), (2) Tú se lo vas a ofrecer (a Noelia) / Tú vas a ofrecérselo (a Noelia), (3) Tú se lo estás ofreciendo (a Fran) / Tú estás ofreciéndoselo (a Fran).

VERBOS REFLEXIVOS (VERBO + PRONOMBRE REFLEXIVO)
REFLEXIVE VERBS (VERB + REFLEXIVE PRONOUN)

When the person performing an action is also the recipient (Verb + Oneself). The Reflexive Pronoun (RP) "brings" the action back to the person who is doing that action. Comparing it with the Object Pronoun: when someone does something and someone else is the recipient, use an Object Pronoun (OP); when someone does something and the same person is the recipient, use a Reflexive Pronoun (RP). There is a Subject-RP-Verb Agreement.

*Reflexive Pronouns (RP)

Person	S	P
1	me (myself)	nos (ourselves)
2	te (yourself)	os (yourselves)
	se (yourself)	se (yourselves)
3	se (him/herself)	se (themselves)

*NOTE: The RPs are exactly the same as the IOPs in a 2OP setting. (See: Indirect Object Pronouns)

As we know, the Subject agrees with the Verb (the action performed by the subject). If someone else is the recipient (IO), then:

Yo te sirvo la cena. (I serve you dinner):
1   2   1

Subject and Verb Agree (Yo sirvo); both 1st Person.
Someone else is the recipient: you, 2nd Person. IOP: te.

But if the subject is the recipient (Reflexive), then they all agree:

Yo me sirvo la cena. (I serve myself dinner):
1   1   1

Subject and Verb Agree (Yo sirvo); both 1st Person.
The subject is also the recipient: I, 1st Person. IOP: me.

The three cases seen in the Object Pronouns apply to the Reflexives:

1. When the verb is **Conjugated**, the RP is placed before the verb.

2. When the verb is in **Infinitive** (in a 2-verb structure: the 1st one is conjugated, the 2nd one is in infinitive), the RP is (a) placed before the conjugated verb, or (b) attached to the end of the infinitive. (See: Additional Sentence Structures)

3. When the verb is in **Gerund** (in a 2-verb structure: the 1st one is conjugated, the 2nd one is in gerund), the RP is (a) placed before the conjugated verb, or (b) attached to the end of the gerund. (See: Present Progressive / Gerund)

To conjugate a reflexive verb, find the reflexive pronoun "se" (oneself) at the end of the verb (after ar, er, ir), replace it with the corresponding pronoun you need (for the recipient, which happens to also be the subject), and place it either before the verb (separately) or after the verb (together), based on the three different cases below. The verb is conjugated as usual.

1. When Reflexive Verbs are Conjugated

(Infinitive + Oneself)
Ex: Cortarse (To cut oneself; to wound oneself accidentally)

Me corto (I cut myself)   Nos cortamos (We cut ourselves)
Te cortas (You cut yourself)   Os cortáis (You cut yourselves)
Se corta (You cut yourself)   Se cortan (You cut yourselves)
Se corta   Se cortan
(He/She cut him/herself)   (They cut themselves)

Note that the **Subject**, the **RP** and the **Verb** all agree (same person): Yo me corto, Tú te cortas, etc.

2. <u>When Reflexive Verbs are in Infinitive</u>

[Cepillarse = to brush oneself]

(a) <u>Nos</u> <u>debemos cepillar</u> los dientes. (We must brush our teeth)

(b) Debemos cepillar<u>nos</u> los dientes.

[Lavarse = to wash oneself]

(a) <u>Se</u> tienen que lavar las manos. (You (all) have to wash your hands)

(b) Tienen que lavar<u>se</u> las manos.

Note the possessive adjectives "our" and "your" in English, but not in Spanish, because Spanish uses the verb in reflexive establishing "whose teeth" and "whose hands", and English does not.

3. <u>When Reflexive Verbs are in Gerund</u>

[Despertándo<u>se</u> = waking up <u>oneself</u>;
Durmiéndo<u>se</u> = falling asleep <u>oneself</u>]

¿<u>Se</u> <u>está</u> durmiendo? (Is he/she falling asleep?)
¿<u>Está</u> durmiéndo<u>se</u>?

- No, <u>se</u> <u>está</u> despertando (No, he/she is waking up)
- No, <u>está</u> despertándo<u>se</u>

Other Uses:

Reflexive Verbs combined with Indirect Object Pronouns

We have seen Double Object Pronouns in a sentence:
IOP – DOP – Verb. (See: Object Pronouns / 2OP)

Reflexive Verbs can be combined with Indirect Object Pronouns in a sentence. As it is usual for conjugated verbs, the Reflexive or the Object pronoun is placed before the verb. In these cases, where both are used, the RP goes first. The order is: RP-IOP-V.

The general message in this sentence structure is: (a) an action happens by itself (Reflexive) to something/someone (3rd Person): "The ice cream melted", (b) on someone's watch (Any Person): "when you/he/she had it". The RP for 3rd Person is "se", and the one who is present when the event happens could be anyone, represented by the appropriate IOP: **Se - Indirect Object Pronoun - Verb**

[pan = bread; quemar<u>se</u> = to burn <u>itself</u> ; me = on my watch]

El pan <u>se</u> <u>me</u> quemó.
     3 1   3

- se quemó (got burned/burned itself) – 3rd Person.
- me (on my watch / when I was in charge of it) – 1st Person.

"The bread got burned (or burned itself) when I was toasting it."

Impersonal "se"

The person performing the action is not established:

Se habla español / "Spanish is spoken (here)" = We speak Spanish
Se vende hielo / "Ice is sold (here)" = We sell ice
Se ofrecen clases de español / "Spanish classes are offered (here)"
Se necesitan empleados / "Employees are needed" = We are hiring

GUSTAR
(To like)

This verb requires some attention because Spanish "gustar" and English "to like" mean the same thing and are used in the same situations, but they work in "opposite directions". The subject and the object are exchanged.
(See: Object Pronouns & Pronouns after Prepositions)

Person	S	P
1	Gusto	Gustamos
2	Gustas	Gustáis
	Gusta	Gustan
3	Gusta	Gustan

Ex: **I like music = Me gusta la música**

After learning about subject pronouns and verbs "living in harmony" and agreement: Yo veo (I see), Tú ves (You see), etc., a very frequent (and logical) question is: Why "Me gusta" and not "Yo gusto"?

In order to understand why, let's see **How It Works**; or you can skip this part and go the next section: **How To Work** with "gustar".

How It Works

In the example above, "I" is the subject, "like" is the action performed by the subject (so they agree accordingly: I like, You like, etc.), and "music" is a Direct Object. If we remember the Object Pronouns, we know we can rephrase it as: I like <u>it</u> (See: Direct Object Pronouns).

But in Spanish, "música" is the subject (3rd Person-Singular) performing the action of "gustar (being likable/pleasant)", and "I" am the recipient, "to me = a mí", so I am an Indirect Object, and the appropriate Indirect Object Pronoun is "me".
(See: Indirect Object Pronouns)

Let's see that in full, in the order that we normally see a sentence, starting with the Subject, "música", (But it is never said this way):

La música gusta a <u>mí</u>* (Music is likable/pleasant to me)

[*Remember: The Personal Subject Pronouns "yo" and "tú" change when they are after Prepositions (a, de, etc.): **yo → mí**, and tú → te] (See: Personal Pronouns after Prepositions)

Replacing the IO with an IOP (which is a correct way to use "gustar"):

La música <u>me</u> gusta (a mí).

And another correct and more common way is (as we started):

Me gusta la música = I like music

As usual, the verb matches with the subject (in Spanish the subject is "música" and in English is "I"): "gustar" with "música", and "to like" with "I". Therefore, when the Subject is plural, "canciones", "gustar" goes in plural:

Me gusta<u>n</u> tus <u>canciones</u> (I like your songs).

How To Work With "Gustar"

After all, it is not that hard to do. We can take it as we see it (even though we are clear that they work in different ways and "I" means "yo", not "me"):
"Me gusta la música" and "I like music" follow the same order.

(1) "Me" and "I", (2) "gusta" and "like", and (3) "la música" and "music".

Just replace the Personal Pronouns (yo, tú, él/ella, etc.) with Object Pronouns (me, te, le, etc., respectively). Plus, remember that "gustar" agrees with whatever it is that you like: music, coffee, pizza, etc., in singular or plural, so it is going to be "gusta" or "gustan".

Te <u>gusta</u> <u>el verbo</u> gustar. (You like the verb "gustar")
Me <u>gustan</u> <u>los idiomas</u>. (I like languages)

If instead of liking "nouns" (la música, el verbo, los idiomas), we like "actions" (estudiar, dormir), the singular form "gusta" is the only one used, even when referring to various actions:

Te <u>gusta</u> <u>estudiar</u> este tema. (You like to study this topic)
Me <u>gusta</u> <u>hablar, leer y escribir</u>. (I like to speak, read and write)

These two other verbs are very common and work exactly like Gustar:
Encantar, Fascinar = **Gustar mucho** (to like very much / a lot)

Me gustan los deportes. (I like sports)
Me <u>gustan mucho</u> los deportes. (I like sports very much)
Me <u>encantan</u> los deportes.
Me <u>fascinan</u> los deportes.

Now, the Long Form. See the table below and get familiarized with the combination: **Pronouns after "A"** and **Indirect Object Pronouns**:

	Pron.		*IOP*		Gustar	
	S	**P**	*S*	*P*	**S**	**P**
1	A mí	A nosotros/as	*me*	*nos*	Gusto	Gustamos
2	A ti	A vosotros/as	*te*	*os*	Gustas	Gustáis
	A usted	A ustedes	*le*	*les*	Gusta	Gustan
3	A él/ella	A ellos/as	*le*	*les*	**Gusta**	**Gustan**

(A mí) me
(A ti) te
(A ud.) **le**
(A él/ella) **le**   + Gusta / Gustan
(A nosotros) nos
(A vosotros) os
(A uds.) **les**
(A ellos/as) **les**

Even though there is redundancy and it might not be required (as seen so far), the use of the long form is common, everywhere. But, you actually need it **to change the person** "liking" something, or **to specify who** that person is when using an ambiguous IOP: le (**Ud. or Él/Ella?**) and les (**Uds. or Ellos/as?**).

A ti te gusta nadar pero a mí me gusta correr.
(You like to swim but I like to run)

A ella le gusta el español. (She likes Spanish)
Without "A ella" we would not know who likes it: Usted? Él? Ella?

A ustedes les encanta la gramática pero a nosotros no nos gusta.
(You all like grammar a lot but we do not like it)

1st and 2nd Persons

So far, everything "being liked" has been in 3rd person (talking **about** music, sports, etc.). When we are in a conversation (I talk **to** you and you talk **to** me) we both have priority and appear at the beginning of the sentence, even when any of the two (or both), 1st or 2nd person, is the one "likable/pleasant". Now we use "gustar" in any other conjugation:

A ti te gusta **ella**. (You like her) / **Tú** le gustas a ella. (She likes you)
As usual, the verb agrees with the subject: "gusta"--"ella", and "gustas"--"tú"; and the IOP agrees with the object: "te"--"a ti" and "le"--"a ella".

A nosotros nos gusta ella. (We like her)

Nosotros le gustamos a ella. (She likes us)

PRETÉRITO: PERFECTO e IMPERFECTO (Indicativo) / PAST TENSE: THE PRETERIT and THE IMPERFECT (Indicative)

There are two main Past Tenses: "Pretérito Perfecto", popularly known as "The Preterit", and "Pretérito Imperfecto", known as "The Imperfect".

Pretérito Perfecto ("The Preterit")

Person	ar		er / ir	
	S	P	S	P
1	-é	-amos	-í	-imos
2	-aste	-asteis	-iste	-isteis
	-ó	-aron	-ió	-ieron
3	-ó	-aron	-ió	-ieron

One general use of the Perfect form is when an event happened once or at a specific time.

[viajar = to travel; comer = to eat; asistir = to attend]

Tú viajaste a Suiza en diciembre.
(You traveled to Switzerland in December)

Samper comió a las 7 de la noche.
(Samper ate at 7pm)

Ellos asistieron a clase anoche.
(They attended class last night)

As always, there are **Irregular Verbs**. Showing some important ones:

*__Ir__: fui, fuiste, fue, fuimos, fuisteis, fueron
*__Ser__: fui, fuiste, fue, fuimos, fuisteis, fueron
Estar: estuve, estuviste, estuvo, estuvimos, estuvisteis, estuvieron
Tener: tuve, tuviste, tuvo, tuvimos, tuvisteis, tuvieron
Poder: pude, pudiste, pudo, pudimos, pudisteis, pudieron
Hacer: hice, hiciste, hizo, hicimos, hicisteis, hicieron
Venir: vine, viniste, vino, vinimos, vinisteis, vinieron
Haber: hubo (As a main verb: There was/were)

*Ir and Ser are spelled identically in the Preterit.
(See: Confusing Verbs)

Pretérito Imperfecto ("The Imperfect")

Person	-ar		-er / -ir	
	S	P	S	P
1	-aba	-ábamos	-ía	-íamos
2	-abas	-abais	-ías	-íais
	-aba	-aban	-ía	-ían
3	-aba	-aban	-ía	-ían

A general way to use the Imperfect form is when an event happened repeatedly (I used to + V) or during a period of time (I was + V-ing).

[viajar = to travel; comer = to eat; asistir = to attend]

Tú viajabas a Suiza en diciembre.
(You used to travel to Switzerland in December)

Samper comía a las 7 de la noche. (Samper used to eat at 7pm)

Ellos asistían a clase de noche. (They used to attend class at night)

Soler / Acostumbrar + Infinitive
(See: Additional Sentence Structures)

Another way to convey "I used to" (Conjugate the first verb in Imperfect and keep the second one in Infinitive):

Solía/Acostumbraba viajar/comer/asistir...
(I used to travel/eat/attend...)

Irregular Verbs:
Ir: iba, ibas, iba, íbamos, ibais, iban
Ser: era, eras, era, éramos, erais, eran
Ver: veía, veías, veía, veíamos, veíais, veían

Preterit & Imperfect combined

This combination is about an event happening (time elapsing) in the past, and sometime within that period another event happened, as an interruption:

[caminar = to walk; ver = to see; quemarse = to burn itself; llegar = to arrive]

Mientras caminaba en el parque, vi un accidente.
(While walking in the park, I saw an accident).

El parque se quemaba cuando llegaron los bomberos.
(The park was burning when the firemen arrived)

Verbs in Past Participle have different uses, as **Adjectives** to describe things or people, combined with "to be" to form the **Passive Voice**, and combined with an auxiliary verb to form **Compound Tenses**.

The verb ending is dropped and one of the following new endings is used instead. There is Gender & Number (G & N) Agreement:

ar: <u>ado</u>* / ada / ados / adas
er/ir: <u>ido</u>* / ida / idos / idas

*Participles in Compound Tenses only use "-ado" or "-ido".
No G & N Agreement. (See: Compound Tenses)

But, if it is not the Preterit or the Imperfect, which Past exactly is the Past Participle? A good way to have a better picture is by revisiting "the past", when learning grammar in school:

Present / Past / **Past Participle**

(I) take / (I) took / **taken**
(yo) tomo / (yo) tomé / **tom<u>ado</u>**

(you) know / (you) knew / **known**
(tú) sabes / (tú) supiste / **sab<u>ido</u>**

1. As Adjectives
(G & N Agreement: Article-Noun-Adj.)

Nouns, and anything related to them, deal with Gender and Number. Adjectives modify nouns, and nouns sometimes come accompanied by Articles.

Las casas pintadas están al final de la calle.
     n.   adj.

(The painted houses are at the end of the street)
     adj.   n.

Note that the article "las", the noun "casas" and the participle (adjective) "pintadas" agree in G & N: Feminine-Plural

¿Podría traerme una papa asada?
     noun adj.

(Could you bring me a (one) baked potato?)
     adj. noun

Note that the article "una", the noun "papa" and the participle (adj.) "asada" agree in G & N: Feminine-Singular

2. Passive Voice
(To be + Participle).
(Agreement: Noun - To Be - Participle).

This form is impersonal. Something was done to the subject, but it is not required to establish "who" did it. Including that information is optional and appears in the sentence after "por" (by). Other information can also be included, like "to/for whom" was done, or other specifications (following a variety of prepositions: de, en, con, bajo, etc).

The Noun and the Participle agree in G & N, and "To be" is conjugated (in any tense) according to the noun, not to the person who actually performed the action, who might not even appear in the sentence. (See: To Be)

Las <u>casas</u> <u>fueron</u> <u>pintadas</u> de azul.
      n.   "ser" participle

(The <u>houses</u> <u>were</u> <u>painted</u> in blue)
        n.   "to be" part.

Note that the article "las", the noun "casas" and the participle "pintadas" agree in G & N: Fem-Plural, and the verb agrees with the noun: 3rd Person-Plural, not with the person who performed the action of painting. We know that the houses were painted, and we know additional information like the color (blue), but we do not know "who" painted them.

La <u>papa</u> <u>fue</u> <u>asada</u> por el cocinero.
      n.   "ser" part.

(The <u>potato</u> <u>was</u> <u>baked</u> by the cook)
        n.   "to be" part.

Besides the usual article-noun-verb-participle agreement observed before, here we know not only that the potato was baked, but also "who" baked it (after "por" / "by"). But again, the verb "fue" (from "ser") agrees with the noun "papa" (3rd P – Singular), not with "the cook" who actually baked it.

3. <u>Compound Tenses</u>
(Auxiliary Verb + Participle)
(See: Compound Tenses)

FUTURO / FUTURE
(Will + Verb)

A common way to express future actions is by using the combination "ir a + infinitivo" (going to + infinitive), which actually conjugates a verb in present tense. The actual Future Tense is sometimes used for more formal expressions, but not necessarily.

Conveniently, the entire set of endings is the same for all three infinitives:
ar, er, ir

Person	S	P
1	-é	-emos
2	-ás	-éis
	-á	-án
3	-á	-án

The way to conjugate verbs in the Future Tense is a little different than the Present and the Past. Simply, add the new ending to the entire verb in infinitive (there is **no need to drop** the infinitive endings: **ar, er, ir**):

Infinitive + Future ending

Estudiar (to study)

Person	S	P
1	Estudiaré (I will study)	Estudiaremos (We will study)
2	Estudiarás (You will study)	Estudiaréis (You will study)
	Estudiará	Estudiarán
3	Estudiará (He/She will study)	Estudiarán (They will study)

Entender (to understand)

Person	S	P
1	Entenderé (I will understand)	Entenderemos
2	Entenderás	Entenderéis
	Entenderá	Entenderán
3	Entenderá	Entenderán

Resumir (to summarize)

Person	S	P
1	Resumiré (I will summarize)	Resumiremos
2	Resumirás	Resumiréis
	Resumirá	Resumirán
3	Resumirá	Resumirán

Irregular Verbs in Future Tense

Tener (to have)

Person	S	P
1	Tendré	Tendremos
2	Tendrás	Tendréis
	Tendrá	Tendrán
3	Tendrá	Tendrán

Querer (to want / to love)

Person	S	P
1	Querré	Querremos
2	Querrás	Querréis
	Querrá	Querrán
3	Querrá	Querrán

Saber (to know)

Person	S	P
1	Sabré	Sabremos
2	Sabrás	Sabréis
	Sabrá	Sabrán
3	Sabrá	Sabrán

Hacer (to do/ to make)

Person	S	P
1	Haré	Haremos
2	Harás	Haréis
	Hará	Harán
3	Hará	Harán

<u>Wondering (present) with the Future Tense</u>

¿Quién <u>será</u>?
(Who would that be? / Lit: "Who <u>will be</u>?)

¿Quién <u>tocará</u> la puerta ahora?
(Who would be knocking on the door now? /
Lit: "Who <u>will knock</u> on the door now?")

¿Qué hora <u>será</u>? (What time would possibly be? /
Lit: "What time <u>will be</u>?")

CONDICIONAL / CONDITIONAL
(Would + Verb)

This tense expresses that an event "could occur" (maybe not) depending on a certain condition (might not be expressed in sentence). Instead of giving "assurance", ("will" happen), something has the "potential" to happen ("would" happen). (For **expressed condition**, See: **Conditional Sentences**)

Like the Future Tense, the endings set is the same for all three infinitives and the conjugation is also done by adding the new ending to the entire verb in infinitive (there is **no need to drop** the infinitive endings: **ar, er, ir**):

Person	S	P
1	-ía	-íamos
2	-ías	-íais
	-ía	-ían
3	-ía	-ían

Estudiar
Yo estudiaría, Tú estudiarías, etc.

Entender
Yo entendería, Tú entenderías, etc.

Resumir
Yo resumiría, Tú resumirías, etc.

Irregular Verbs in Conditional Tense

The irregular verbs in the Future Tense are also irregulars in the Conditional, with the same spelling changes. Add the appropriate Conditional endings shown in the Table.
(See: Irregular Verbs in Future)

Tener
Yo tendría, Tú tendrías, etc.

Querer
Yo querría, Tú querrías, etc.

Saber
Yo sabría, Tú sabrías, etc.

Hacer
Yo haría, Tú harías, etc.

IMPERATIVO / IMPERATIVE (COMMANDS)
(with Object Pronouns)

Tool: a ⇔ e

When a verb is conjugated in Present Tense (Indicative), we can observe an "a" pattern (ar verbs) and an "e" pattern (er/ir verbs). In many cases, an exchange is required to form the Imperative: from a to e or from e to a.

Examples:

Ordenar = to order : "a" pattern

Person	S	P
1	ordeno	ordenamos
2	ordenas	ordenáis
	ordena	ordenan
3	ordena	ordenan

For the "Tú" and "Vosotros" forms:

- Tú: Use the conjugation in Present Indicative but dropping the "s" at the end, like in the Usted form or 3rd person singular (él/ella).
Vosotros: Replace the endings "-áis, -éis, -ís" with "-ad, -ed, -id" (from ar, er, ir, respectively).

- For the negative command, use the same conjugation for "tú" and "vosotros" in Present Indicative, using the a⇔e exchange.

Tú: Ordena la comida. / No ordenes la comida.

Vosotros: Ordenad la comida. / No ordenéis la comida.

For Usted, Ustedes and Nosotros:

- Just do the a⇔e exchange.

- For the Negative, the verb in Affirmative Command does not change, just add "no" before it.

Usted: Order<u>e</u> la comida. / No order<u>e</u> la comida.

Ustedes: Orden<u>e</u>n la comida. / No orden<u>e</u>n la comida.

Nosotros: Orden<u>e</u>mos la comida. / No orden<u>e</u>mos la comida.

Comer = to eat : "e" pattern

Person	S	P
1	como	com**e**mos
2	com**es**	com**é**is
	com**e**	com**e**n
3	com**e**	com**e**n

Tú and Vosotros:

Tú: Com<u>e</u> / No com<u>as</u>

Vosotros: Com<u>ed</u> / No com<u>á</u>is

Usted, Ustedes and Nosotros:

Usted: Com<u>a</u> / No com<u>a</u>

Ustedes: Com<u>an</u> / No com<u>an</u>

Nosotros: Com<u>a</u>mos / No com<u>a</u>mos

Irregular Commands
(See: Verbs with Spelling Changes)

Ir (to go)

Tú: Ve / No vayas
Vosotros: Id / No vayáis
Usted: Vaya / No vaya
Ustedes: Vayan / No vayan
Nosotros: Vayamos / No vayamos

Venir (to come)

Tú: Ven / No vengas
Vosotros: Venid / No vengáis
Usted: Venga / No venga
Ustedes: Vengan / No vengan
Nosotros: Vengamos / No vengamos

Poner (to put)

Tú: Pon / No pongas
Vosotros: Poned / No pongáis
Usted: Ponga / No ponga
Ustedes: Pongan / No pongan
Nosotros: Pongamos / No pongamos

Salir (to go out / to get out / to exit)

Tú: Sal / No salgas
Vosotros: Salid / No salgáis
Usted: Salga / No salga
Ustedes: Salgan / No salgan
Nosotros: Salgamos / No salgamos

Commands with Object Pronouns

- Object Pronouns can be used with Commands, attached to the end of the verb (in reversed order when using double pronouns: IOP-DOP). (See: Double Object Pronouns)

- For Negative Commands, the Pronouns go before the verb, separately.

1. (Tú) Compra café para ella (Buy coffee for her)

Cómpra<u>selo</u>   →   No <u>se</u> <u>lo</u> compres
      IOP-DOP   IOP-DOP

2. (Ud.) Compre café para ella. (Buy coffee for her)

Cómpre<u>selo</u>   →   No <u>se</u> <u>lo</u> compre

3. (Uds.) Compren café para ella

Cómpren<u>selo</u>   →   No <u>se</u> <u>lo</u> compren

4. (Nosotros) Compremos café para ella

Comprémo<u>selo</u>   →   No <u>se</u> <u>lo</u> compremos

5. (Vosotros) Comprad café para ella

Comprád<u>selo</u>   →   No <u>se</u> <u>lo</u> compréis

While the Present Indicative expresses a fact or statement (Rocío estudia mucho / Rocío studies a lot), the **Present Subjunctive** normally reflects **uncertainty** (looking towards the future) within many different situations and moods, like: **Doubt, Preference, Wish/Desire, Hope, Request, Advice, Probability, Necessity, and others.**

Presente Subjuntivo (Present Subjunctive)

Person	ar		er/ir	
	S	P	S	P
1	-e	-emos	-a	-amos
2	-es	-éis	-as	-áis
	-e	-en	-a	-an
3	-e	-en	-a	-an

Just like the Imperative in "Usted" form, **there is an a⇔e exchange** between the Indicative and the Subjunctive but for **all conjugations**. (See: Imperative)

Estudiar (to study)
Indicative: estudio, estudias, estudia, estudiamos, estudiáis, estudian
Subjunctive: estudie, estudies, estudie, estudiemos, estudiéis, estudien

Leer (to read)
Indic.: leo, lees, lee, leemos, leéis, leen
Subj.: lea, leas, lea, leamos, leáis, lean

Escribir (to write)
Indic.: escribo, escribes, escribe, escribimos, escribís, escriben
Subj.: escriba, escribas, escriba, escribamos, escribáis, escriban

A common characteristic of the Subjunctive is the existence of **two subjects** in the sentence (change of subject), each one doing a different action (**two verbs**). In the Present Subjunctive tense, the first subject acts "now" and the second one is supposed to act "later". The first verb appears in Present Indicative and followed by "que" (that), which introduces the change of subject and its verb in Subjunctive.

In the Present Subjunctive, there are many cases where there is only one subject, but the sentence does reflect a future action:

Llama (tú) cuando termines (tú).
(Call (you) whenever (future) you finish)

Some of the **verbs in Indicative introducing the Subjunctive** are:

Esperar (to hope, to expect)
Desear (to wish)
Dudar (to doubt)
Necesitar (to need)
Querer (to want)   +   **que**
Preferir (to prefer)
Pedir (to request, to ask for)
Aconsejar (to advise)

Ojalá (not a verb) is an expression of hope/wish widely used in all Spanish-speaking countries. Followed by "que" works with the Subjunctive.

Note the Indicative verb at the beginning in present tense, and the Subjunctive in present too. Also note a change of subjects with two different actions in the same sentence ("Showing literal English equivalent"):

Ind.: Tú <u>estudias</u> mucho. (You study a lot)
Sub: Yo <u>espero que</u> tú <u>estudies</u> mucho.
("I hope that you study a lot")

I: Ellos <u>leen</u> el libro. (They read the book)
S: El profesor <u>desea que</u> ellos <u>lean</u> el libro.
("The professor wishes that they read the book")

I: Yo <u>escribo</u> demasiado. (I write too much)
S: Ustedes <u>prefieren que</u> yo <u>escriba</u> menos.
("You prefer that I write less")

With **no change of subject**, so the person "hoping, wishing, etc" is the same person who should perform the second action in the sentence, there is no need for Subjunctive conjugation (and no "que" introducing it). It would be a double verb where the first one is conjugated (in present tense) and the second one remains in infinitive. (See: Additional Sentence Structures)

Yo <u>espero estudiar</u> mucho.
El profesor <u>desea leer</u> el libro.
Ustedes <u>prefieren escribir</u> menos.

[entender = to understand]
<u>Ojalá que</u> entend<u>as</u> todo.
("It is hoped" that you understand everything)

PRETÉRITO IMPERFECTO (SUBJUNTIVO) / IMPERFECT (SUBJUNCTIVE)

Just like the Present Indicative compares to the Present Subjunctive, the Past Indicative compares to the Imperfect Subjunctive. While a past tense in Indicative expresses a fact or statement (Rocío estudiaba mucho / Rocío used to study a lot), the Imperfect Subjunctive normally reflects uncertainty within many different situations and moods, like: **Doubt, Preference, Wish/Desire, Hope, Request, Advice, Probability, Necessity, and others.**

Imperfecto Subjuntivo (Imperfect Subjunctive)

Person	ar S	ar P	er/ir S	er/ir P
1	-ara/-ase	-áramos/ -ásemos	-iera/-iese	-iéramos/ -iésemos
2	-aras/-ases -ara/-ase	-arais/-aseis -aran/-asen	-ieras/-ieses -iera/-iese	-ierais/-ieseis -ieran/-iesen
3	-ara/-ase	-aran/-asen	-iera/-iese	-ieran/-iesen

(Notice the two different ending patterns)

A common characteristic of the Subjunctive is the existence of **two subjects** in the sentence (change of subject), each one doing a different action (**two verbs**). In the Imperfect Subjunctive tense, both actions belong to the past. The first verb appears in Past Indicative and followed by "que" (that), which introduces the change of subject and its verb in Subjunctive.

Some of the **verbs in Indicative introducing the Subjunctive** are:

Esperar (to hope, to expect)
Desear (to wish)
Dudar (to doubt)
Necesitar (to need)
Querer (to want)   +   **que**
Preferir (to prefer)
Pedir (to request, to ask for)
Aconsejar (to advise)

Note the Indicative verb at the beginning in past tense, and the Subjunctive in past too. Also note a change of subjects with two different actions in the same sentence ("Showing literal English equivalent"):

ar
I: Rocío <u>estudiaba</u> mucho. (Rocío used to study a lot)
S: Yo <u>esperaba</u> que Rocío <u>estudiara</u> mucho.
("I hoped that Rocío studied a lot")

er
I: Rocío leyó el libro. (Rocío read the book)
S: El profesor <u>deseaba</u> que Rocío <u>leyera</u> el libro.
("The professor wished that Rocío read the book")

ir
I: El profesor <u>escribía</u> demasiado.
(The professor used to write too much)
S: Rocío <u>prefería</u> que el profesor <u>escribiera</u> menos.
("Rocío preferred that the professor wrote less")

When there is **no change of subject**, so the person who "hoped, wished, etc" is the same person who performed (or not) the second action in the sentence, there is no need for Subjunctive conjugation (and no "que" introducing it). It would be a double verb where the first one is conjugated (in past tense) and the second one remains in infinitive.
(See: Additional Sentence Structures)

Yo <u>esperaba estudiar</u> mucho.
El profesor <u>deseaba leer</u> el libro.
Rocío <u>prefería escribir</u> menos.

Comparing the **Present Subjunctive**...

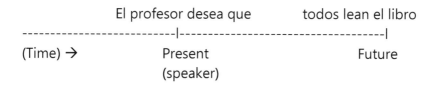

El profesor desea que   todos lean el libro

```
-----------------------------|----------------------------------|
(Time) →              Present                        Future
                     (speaker)
```

...with the **Imperfect Subjunctive**

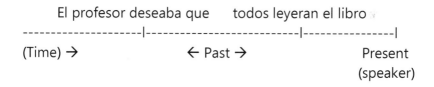

El profesor deseaba que   todos leyeran el libro

```
--------------------|---------------------------|----------------|
(Time) →                        ← Past →                Present
                                                       (speaker)
```

Some of the English and Spanish names for these tenses do not match word by word, so they could be confusing. For instance, in English the term "Perfect" basically refers to a tense with two verbs (Auxiliary + Participle), which is not the case in Spanish. In Spanish, the amount of verbs in a tense is normally defined as "Simple" (Simple) = one verb, or "Compound" (Compuesto) = more than one verb.

Therefore, Past Perfect refers to a Compound form of a Past Tense: I had seen = Yo había visto

But, in Spanish, Pretérito Perfecto is a Simple Tense: Yo vi =I saw

And its Compound version is called Pretérito Perfecto Compuesto: Yo he visto = I have seen (called Present Perfect in English)

Another example is the Future Perfect. Again, it is a Compound Tense: She will have gone = Ella habrá ido

In Spanish this tense is called Futuro Compuesto.

Among other uses, "**Haber**" also works as an **Auxiliary** verb to form compound tenses when combined with Participles, like in English when "have" is used as an auxiliary verb for the same purpose, in which case "to have" does not mean "to possess". (See: Haber)

The **Auxiliary** verb "Haber" is conjugated as usual, according to the subject. The **Participle** remains in its Singular-Masculine ending form: **-ado or -ido** (from "ar" verbs or "er/ir" verbs, respectively). (No Gender & Number Agreement)

Do not get confused:
Haber (main verb) = existence/presence: Hay = There is/are
Haber (auxiliary) = To have (auxiliary)
Tener = To have (main verb)

The name does not translate word by word, "Pretérito" Perfecto and "Present" Perfect. The auxiliary verb is in present tense (therefore the name in English is "Present"), but the whole compound tense is in the past (therefore the name in Spanish is "Pretérito"). This tense is commonly used to refer to past events that have happened more than once or during a length of time, and it could be thought of as "and counting" or "as of today".

Also, it is used when referring to just one event that happened recently (almost now), commonly in Spain but not so much in Latin America (where the Preterit Perfect Simple (The Preterit) is normally used instead).
(See: Preterit)

Haber (Present Ind.)

Person	S	P
1	he	hemos
2	has	habéis
	ha	han
3	ha	han

Sofy <u>ha</u> <u>ofrecido</u> muchos seminarios. (repeatedly, and counting)
  (Aux) (Participle)

(Sofy <u>has</u> <u>offered</u> many seminars)

Tito <u>ha</u> <u>sido</u> director por muchos años. (length of time, as of today)
(Tito <u>has</u> <u>been</u> a director for many years)

Ellos <u>han</u> <u>llegado</u> del trabajo. (almost now)
(They <u>have</u> <u>arrived</u> from work)

When talking about two events in the past, this tense refers to the one that occurred first (past from a past event).
(See: Imperfect & Participle)

Haber (Imperfect Indicative)

Person	S	P
1	había	habíamos
2	habías	habíais
	había	habían
3	había	habían

[Nydia goes somewhere and her cousin Pam has not called yet]

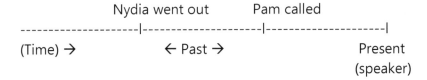

Nydia <u>había</u> <u>salido</u> cuando Pam <u>llamó</u>.
  (Imperfect) (Participle)

(Nydia <u>had</u> <u>gone out</u> when Pam <u>called</u>)

Note the two events in the past, "Nydia went out" and "Pam called". The one that occurred first is in Pluperfect Compound, "Nydia <u>had gone</u> out", before "Pam called".

Ellas <u>no habían acordado</u> nada el día anterior.
  (Pluperfect Compound)

(They <u>had not agreed</u> on anything the day before)

When dealing with two events in the future, this tense refers to the one that occurs first. The first future event is in the past of a second future event. Auxiliary "Haber" in Future + Main Verb in Participle (Will have + Participle). (See: Future & Participle)

Haber (Future)

Person	S	P
1	habré	habremos
2	habrás	habréis
	habrá	habrán
3	habrá	habrán

[Navi will eat at 9:00]

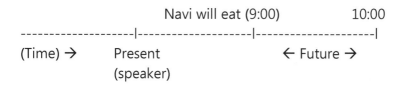

```
                        Navi will eat (9:00)            10:00
-------------------|--------------------|--------------------|
(Time) →      Present                        ← Future →
              (speaker)
```

Navi <u>habrá comido</u> antes de las 10:00.
(Navi <u>will have eaten</u> before 10:00)

Note that "Navi will eat" and "10:00" are both in the future. The one that will occur first is in Future Perfect (Futuro Compuesto), "Navi <u>will have eaten</u>" before 10:00.

Todos <u>habrán cenado</u> a las 10:00.
(Everyone <u>will have eaten dinner</u> by 10:00)

This tense refers to an event that could have happened after (future of) a previous event (should this one had (or not) occurred). Auxiliary "Haber" in Conditional + Main Verb in Participle (Would have + Participle). (See: Conditional & Participle)

Haber (Conditional)

Person	S	P
1	habría	habríamos
2	habrías	habríais
	habría	habrían
3	habría	habrían

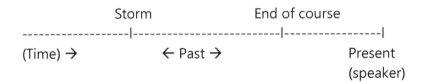

	Storm	End of course

(Time) →   ← Past →   Present
                                    (speaker)

Los estudiantes <u>habrían terminado</u> su curso, pero hubo una tormenta.
(The students <u>would have finished</u> their course, but there was a storm)

Note both events in the past: the "storm" and the "end of course". The second one is expressed in Conditional Perfect, and had the possibility to happen but a previous event did not allow it.

El ingeniero <u>habría hecho</u> el proyecto, pero fue cancelado.
(The engineer <u>would have done</u> the project, but it was canceled)

The Subjunctive Tenses involve different moods like uncertainty and hope, and many times involve a change of subjects and actions. The Present Perfect Subjunctive describes an event "by now" or "later" but before a deadline (which could be a second event). When dealing with two subjects, the first one uses a verb in Indicative followed by "que", introducing the Subjunctive.
(See: Present Subjunctive & Participle)

Haber (Present Subjunctive)

Person	S	P
1	haya	hayamos
2	hayas	hayáis
	haya	hayan
3	haya	hayan

```
              The students learned     The teacher hopes
---------------------|---------------------|
(Time) →          Past                Present
                                      (speaker)
```

("Showing literal English equivalent"):

El maestro <u>espera que</u> los estudiantes <u>hayan aprendido</u>. (by now)
("The teacher <u>hopes that</u> the students <u>have learned</u>")

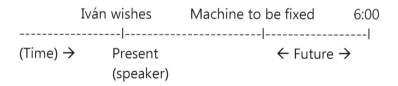

```
           Iván wishes     Machine to be fixed      6:00
-----------------|---------------------------|-----------------|
(Time) →       Present                     ← Future →
               (speaker)
```

Iván <u>desea que</u> la máquina <u>haya funcionado</u> antes de las 6:00. (later)
("Iván <u>wishes that</u> the machine <u>has worked</u> before 6:00")

PRETÉRITO PLUSCUAMPERFECTO (SUBJUNTIVO) / PAST PERFECT (SUBJUNCTIVE): PLUPERFECT (SUBJUNCTIVE)

("Haber" in Imperfect Subjunctive + Participle)

When there are two events in the past, this form of Subjunctive is used to refer to the second one (which happens on the contrary to the expected), after a change of subject.
(See: Imperfect Subjunctive & Participle)

Haber (Imperfect Subjunctive)

Person	S	P
1	hubiera / hubiese	hubiéramos / hubiésemos
2	hubieras / hubieses	hubierais / hubieseis
	hubiera / hubiese	hubieran / hubiesen
3	hubiera / hubiese	hubieran / hubiesen

(Notice the two different ending patterns)

```
          The professor hopes      that his students attend
----------------|----------------------------|----------------|
(Time) →                ← Past →                    Present
                                                    (speaker)
```

("Showing literal English equivalent"):

El profesor <u>esperaba que</u> sus estudiantes <u>hubieran asistido</u> ayer.
("The professor <u>hoped that</u> his students <u>had attended</u> yesterday")

Ellos <u>dudaban</u> que su profesor <u>hubiera estado</u> allí.
("They <u>doubted</u> that their professor <u>had been</u> there")

CONDITIONAL SENTENCES

When the condition is expressed in the sentence, there are different combinations of tenses to do so.

Presente (Indicativo) + Futuro / Present (Indicative) + Future
("If" + Present Ind. + Future)

The condition (introduced by if = "si") should be met "later" in order for a future event to happen. [If (later)..., something will happen]
(See: Present, Future)

Si <u>viajo</u> a Italia, <u>visitaré</u> el Coliseo Romano.
  (Present)   (Future)

(If I <u>travel</u> ("later") to Italy, I <u>will visit</u> the Roman Colosseum)

Si ella <u>practica</u> más, <u>hablará</u> español con fluidez.
(If she <u>practices</u> more, she <u>will speak</u> Spanish fluently)

Imperfecto (Subjuntivo) + Condicional /
Imperfect Subjunctive + Conditional
("If" + Imperf. Subj. + Conditional)

The condition (introduced by if = "si") should be met "by now or later" in order for a future event to happen.
(See: Imperfect Subjunctive, Future Conditional).

Si yo <u>tuviera</u> más tiempo, <u>viajaría</u> frecuentemente.
    (Imp. Subj.)   (Conditional)

(If I <u>had</u> ("by now/later") more time, I <u>would travel</u> ("later") frequently)

Si ella <u>practicara</u> más, <u>hablaría</u> español con fluidez.
(If she <u>practiced</u> more, she <u>would speak</u> Spanish fluently)

Pluscuamperfecto (Subjuntivo) + Condicional Compuesto/
Pluperfect (Subjunctive) + Conditional Perfect
("If" + Pluperfect Subj. + Conditional Perfect)

The condition (introduced by if = "si") has to be met (past) for a second event to happen afterward (also past).
(See: Pluperfect Subj. & Conditional Perfect)

Si <u>hubiera tenido</u> más tiempo, <u>habría viajado</u> frecuentemente.
   (Pluperfect Subj.)   (Conditional Perfect)

(If I had had ("past") more time, I <u>would have traveled</u> ("past") frequently)

Pretérito Perfecto (Indicativo) / Present Perfect (Indicative):
Yo he comido pizza. / I have eaten pizza.

Pretérito Perfecto (Subjuntivo) / Present Perfect (Subjunctive):
Tú esperas que yo haya comido pizza. /
You expect that I have eaten pizza.

Pluscuamperfecto (Indicativo) / Pluperfect (Indicative):
Ella había comprado el libro antes de ir a clase. /
She had bought the book before going to class.

Pluscuamperfecto (Subjuntivo) / Pluperfect (Subjunctive):
Yo esperaba que ella hubiera comprado el libro antes de ir a clase. /
"I expected that she had bought the book before going to class."

Futuro Compuesto (Indicativo) / Future Perfect (Indicative):
Tú habrás terminado tu tarea antes de las 7:00. /
You will have finished your homework before 7:00.

Condicional Compuesto / Conditional Perfect:
Tú habrías terminado tu tarea ya, pero te dormiste. /
You would have finished your homework already, but you fell asleep.

**Progresivo (Gerundio) Compuesto /
Progressive (Gerund) Compound:**
Habiendo dicho eso... / Having said that...

Infinitivo Compuesto / Infinitive Perfect:
Estoy contento de haber encontrado una solución. /
I am glad to have found a solution.

Using both forms of Haber (Auxiliary and Main Verbs)

(Remember: When "haber" means "there is/are" it remains in singular form even for nouns in plural; applicable to Compound Tenses)

<u>Ha habido</u> más ayuda antes. / There <u>has been</u> more help before.

<u>Ha habido</u> más plato<u>s</u> rotos. / There <u>have been</u> more broken dishe<u>s</u>.

(Había habido, Habrá habido, Habría habido, Haya habido, Hubiera habido)

Just like in English "To have", whose two forms (Auxiliary and Main) can appear together as compound tenses:

I have had, I had had, I will have had, I would have had, etc.
(He tenido, Había tenido, Habré tenido, Habría tenido, etc.)

These elements connect words, phrases or sentences, to express more complete ideas. The most common of these "connectors" are:

Pero* (But)
Mas* (But)
Sino* (But)
Porque (Because)
Pues (So, Because)
Que (Than, That)
Como (Because, As)
Aunque (Although, Even though)
Así que (So)
Y (And)
O (Or)
Ni (Neither, Nor)

*Pero / Mas (But)
These two are synonyms, therefore they are exchangeable. Used to express a contrary idea/reason/action:

Starting with an affirmative statement:
(2nd statement refers to a limitation/condition)

Quiero ir a Italia, pero/mas no tengo dinero.
(I want to go to Italy, but I do not have money)

Glenda viaja en barco pero/mas no (viaja) en avión.
(Glenda travels by ship but not by airplane)

Starting with a negative statement:
(The 2nd statement is a fair substitution):

No iré al cine, pero/mas iré al concierto.
(I will not go to the theater, but I will go to the concert)

Glenda no viaja en avión, pero/mas viaja en barco.
(Glenda does not travel by airplane, but she travels by ship)

*Sino (But)
Like Pero and Mas, but only used when starting with a negative statement. It is a little different from Pero/Mas (when starting with a negative statement) because it does not suggest that the 2nd statement is a fair substitution, it just replaces the 1st one.

Él no irá al cine, sino (que irá) a la biblioteca.
(He will not go to the theater, but to the library)

Ella no viaja en avión, sino (que viaja) en barco.
(She does not travel by airplane, but by ship)

Que (Than, That)
Used with the Comparative Adjectives/Adverbs, and to introduce the Subjunctive Mood:

Un avión es <u>más</u> caro <u>que</u> un carro.
(An airplane is <u>more</u> expensive <u>than</u> a car)

<u>Espero que</u> puedas viajar.
(<u>I hope that</u> you can travel)

Porque (Because)
Introduces an explanation or reason:

Nydia estudia mucho porque quiere obtener A.
(Nydia studies a lot because she wants to get an A)

Como (Because, As)

To explain a reason, starting a sentence. Also, used with the Superlative:

Como estudiaron tanto, pasaron la clase con A.
(Because they studied a lot, they passed the class with an A)

Manu es <u>tan</u> inteligente <u>como</u> Nydia.
(Manu is <u>as</u> intelligent <u>as</u> Nydia)

Pues (So, Then)

To express an alternative, or continue with a narration:

Dices que no te gusta viajar en avión; pues, viaja en tren.
(You say you do not like to travel by airplane; so, travel by train)

Así que (So)

It is used to introduce an event that results from another one. Like "for that reason":

La profesora Juana no vino hoy, así que no tenemos clase de historia.
(Professor Juana did not come today, so we do not have History class)

Aunque (Although, Even though)

To express a contrary action that does not affect the 1st one:

Pasaron la clase, aunque no estudiaron mucho.
(They passed the class, although they did not study that much)

Y** (And)

To combine/include two or more elements in a sentence:

Ella es la profesora de historia y de francés.
(She is the History and French professor)

**"E" replaces "Y" when the next word starts with the same "ee" sound:

Ella es la profesora de francés e historia.
(Remember: "h" is silent → "hi-" sounds "ee")
(She is the French and History professor)

O*** (Or)
To present two or more options in a sentence:

¿Qué clase prefieren Manu y Nydia, historia o francés?
(What class do Manu and Nydia prefer, History or French?)

***"U" replaces "O" when the next word starts with the same "oh" sound:

Ellos prefieren redacción u oratoria.
(They prefer composition or public speaking)

Ni (Neither, Nor)
To express two negative elements
(Remember the double negative in Spanish):

Manu y Nydia no quieren ni historia ni francés.
(Manu and Nydia want neither History nor French)

RELATIVOS / RELATIVES
(See: Articles, Prepositions, Pronouns, and Adverbs)

Relatives, just like Conjunctions, connect elements within a sentence. They introduce/connect additional information.

Simple
Pronouns: que (that), quien/quienes (who)
Adjective: cuyo/a/os/as (whose)
Adverbs: donde (where), cuando (when), como (how, like), cuanto (as much as)

Compound
[el, la, los, las] + que (the one/ones), lo + que (what)
[el, la, lo] + cual (which) / [los, las] + cuales (which)

After Prepositions
Preposition + Simple/Compound Relatives

Note: Relatives (que, quien, donde, cuando, como, cuanto) do not need accent marks, as opposed to Question/Exclamation words.

Simple

Que
Introduces information directly related to the subject, as a continuation of it:

El libro de historia que todos leen.
(The History book that everyone reads)

The main topic is "the History book", and then we add some information about it: everyone reads it. "Que" introduces the additional information about the noun "book".

La autora que escribió el libro de historia que todos leen.
(The author that/who wrote the History book that everyone reads)

Quien / Quienes
(Number Agreement – with the Subject)

When the subject is a person, "quien" adds information (not related to the main topic) about the same Subject/Person:

La autora ganó un premio por su obra.
(The author won a prize for her work)

La autora también es actriz.
(The author is also an actress)

La autora, quien también es actriz, ganó un premio por su obra.
(The author, who also is an actress, won a prize for her work)

(Plural: Las autoras, quienes también son actrices, ganaron..)

Being an actress does not affect the fact that the author won a prize for her excellent book. Therefore, the additional unrelated information "quien también es actriz" can be erased and the main sentence is not affected. As we saw before: "La autora ganó un premio por su obra".
(The author won a prize for her work).

Cuyo/Cuya/Cuyos/Cuyas
(Gender & Number Agreement – with a 2ⁿᵈ noun)

These ones introduce another event (which involves a second subject/noun), related to the main one. Cuyo/Cuya/Cuyos/Cuyas agree with the second subject.

La autora también es actriz.
(The author is also an actress)

Su libro de historia ganó un premio.
(Her History book won a prize)

La autora, <u>cuyo libro de historia</u> ganó un premio, también es actriz.
(The author, <u>whose History book</u> won a prize, is also an actress)

"La autora" is the main subject and "libro" is the second one.
"Cuyo" agrees in Gender & Number with "libro" (2nd noun), not with "autora" (main subject).

Again, if the additional information "cuyo libro de historia ganó un premio" is erased, the main sentence is not affected. As we saw before: "La autora también es actriz".

Let's exchange the roles in the sentence to see the difference:

El libro de historia, <u>cuya autora</u> también es actriz, ganó un premio.
(The History book, whose author is also an actress, won an award)

Now, "El libro" is the main subject and "autora" is the second one, and "cuya" agrees with "autora", not with "libro".

Donde (where), Cuando (when), Como (however, as, like), Cuanto (as much as)

Leyeron el libro donde quisieron.
(They read the book where they wanted)

Leyeron el libro cuando quisieron.
(They read the book when they wanted)

Leyeron el libro como quisieron.
(They read the book however they wanted)

Leyeron el libro cuanto quisieron.
(They read the book as much as they wanted)

Compound Pronouns

[el, la, los, las] + que (the one/ones), lo + que (what)
[el, la, lo] + cual (which) / [los, las] + cuales (which)

When the noun is not present (to avoid repetition), the article remains in the sentence along with the relative "que" or "cual/cuales", and agrees in Number with the noun:

¿Quieres el libro de historia que todos leen u otro?
(Do you want the History book that everyone reads or another one?)
- Quiero el que todos leen. (I want the one that everyone reads)

"El" agrees with the noun "libro" (masculine-singular), so none of the other options (la, los, las) can be used.

"Que" and "cual/cuales" are most of the times synonyms, used to specify/clarify the subject by making reference to another event, which is related to the subject. ("cual / cuales" deal with Number agreement – with the Article and the Subject/Noun):

Esos libros, los que/cuales te mencioné ayer, son excelentes.
(Those books, the ones I mentioned to you yesterday, are excellent)

Lo is a neutral article, used when the subject is abstract or absent.
Lo Que = what:

Eso es exactamente lo que quiero. (That is exactly what I want)

- After Prepositions

When combining two sentences, the preposition in the one "to be incorporated" goes along with (and before) the relative in the newly combined sentence:

La profesora escribió una novela. (The professor wrote a novel)

Yo hablé con la profesora ayer. (I spoke with the professor yesterday)

La profesora, <u>con quien hablé</u> ayer, escribió una novela.
(The professor, <u>with whom I spoke</u> yesterday, wrote a novel)

<u>Todos leen el libro</u> con un entusiasmo impresionante.
(<u>Everyone reads the book</u> with an impressive enthusiasm)

If now we make "entusiasmo" the main subject (not "todos"):

<u>El entusiasmo</u> con el que/cual todos leen el libro <u>es impresionante</u>.
(<u>The enthusiasm</u> with which everyone reads the book <u>is impressive</u>)

"El que/cual" follows the preposition from the original sentence: "con".
But now, the "main character" is "entusiasmo" (enthusiasm), not "todos" (everyone), so "el que/cual" agrees with "entusiasmo", not with "todos".

Let's see it by using "alegría" (fem.) instead of "entusiasmo" (masc.):

Todos leen el libro con una alegría impresionante.
(Everyone reads the book with an impressive happiness)

Rephrasing with the Relative after Preposition:
La alegría* con <u>la</u>* que/cual todos leen el libro es impresionante.
(The happiness with which everyone reads the book is impressive)

*Note the feminine "la" agreeing with the feminine "alegría"

But, sometimes "cual / cuales" cannot be replaced by "que", like when the object ("libros", in the example below) is divided into a specific amount when providing the additional information.

Ella compró cuatro libros, <u>dos de los cuales</u> son de español.
(She bought four books, <u>two of which</u>* are about Spanish)
*Two out of the total of books.

In Spanish, some words change their meaning or use by having an accent mark or not. A good example is that monosyllables, as a general rule, do not need an accent mark, but in order to differentiate one meaning from the other, an accent mark is used. Other ones are not monosyllables and work in the same way. Some essential ones are:

Mi (adj.) = My
Mí (pron.) = Me

Tu (adj.) = Your
Tú (pron.) = You

El (art.) = The
Él (pron.) = He

Si (conj.) = If
Sí (adv.) = Yes
Sí (pron.) = Reflexive personal pronoun after preposition, in 3rd Person: Himself/Herself, Themselves: Prep. (a/de/para/por, etc.) + "sí" or "sí mismo".

Se (object or reflexive pron.)
Sé (verb in 1st person-singular) = I know
Sé (command in "tú" form) = Be (you)

Este (adj. / pron. / cardinal point) = This / This one / East)
Éste (pron.) = This one. Accent needed only when avoiding ambiguity:

Ex:
Este (this) punto es norte (north) y el otro punto es este (east).

¿Cuál punto es éste (this one), norte (north) o este (east)?
- Norte.

¿Cuál punto es este (east), éste (this one) o el otro?
- El otro

Ese (letter) = S
Ese (adj. or pron.) = That or that one
Ése (pron.) = That one. Accent needed only when avoiding ambiguity:

Ex:
No sé si su nombre es con "s" o con "z". Escríbelo, por favor. ¿Quieres escribirlo con este bolígrafo o con ese? /
I do not know if his/her name is with an "s" or with a "z". Write it down, please. Do you want to write it with this pen or with that one?

- Voy a escribirlo con ese. /
I am going to write it with... ("s"? or "that one"?)
- Voy a escribirlo con ése. /
I am going to write it with that one.

Solo (adj. / adv.) = Alone / Only
Sólo (adv.) = Only. Accent needed only when avoiding ambiguity:

Ex:
Él quería ir solo al parque. /
He wanted to go alone to the park.

Él quería ir sólo (solamente) al parque. /
He wanted to go only to the park.

Que (rel. pron.) = That
Qué (interrogative/exclamative) = What? / What a...!

Como (v. "to eat", 1st person-singular) = I eat
Como (rel. adv.) = Like (the same way), However (any way)
Cómo (interrogative/exclamative) = How? / How...!

Cual (rel. pron.) = Which
Cuál (interrog./exclam.) = Which? / Tell me which one!

Cuanto/s (rel. adv.) = As much/many as
Cuánto/s (interrog./exclam.) = How much/many? / See how many...!
Quien (rel. adv.) = Who
Quién (interrog./exclam.) = Who? / Look who...!

Donde (rel. adv.) = Where
Dónde (interrog./exclam.) = Where? / Show me where...!

Porque (conj.) = Because
Porqué (noun) = The "why" (the reason)
Por qué (interrog.) = Why?

Aun (adv.) = Even
Aún (adv.) = Still

Ex:
Diez y aun (hasta/incluso) más. / Ten and even more.
¿Estás aún (todavía) leyendo el libro? /
Are you still reading the book?

Ir and Ser

These two irregular verbs are identical in the **Preterit Indicative** and in the **Imperfect Subjunctive**:

Present Indicative

Ir: Voy, Vas, Va, Vamos, Vais, Van
Ser: Soy, Eres, Es, Somos, Sois, Son

Preterit Indicative

Ir		Ser	
Fui	**Fuimos**	**Fui**	**Fuimos**
Fuiste	**Fuisteis**	**Fuiste**	**Fuisteis**
Fue	**Fueron**	**Fue**	**Fueron**
Fue	**Fueron**	**Fue**	**Fueron**

Imperfect Indicative

Ir: Iba, Ibas, Iba, Íbamos, Ibais, Iban
Ser: Era, Eras, Era, Éramos, Erais, Eran

Present Subjunctive

Ir: Vaya, Vayas, Vaya, Vayamos, Vayáis, Vayan
Ser: Sea, Seas, Sea, Seamos, Seáis, Sean

Imperfect Subjunctive

Ir		Ser	
Fuera	**Fuéramos**	**Fuera**	**Fuéramos**
Fueras	**Fuerais**	**Fueras**	**Fuerais**
Fuera	**Fueran**	**Fuera**	**Fueran**
Fuera	**Fueran**	**Fuera**	**Fueran**

Participle: Ido / Sido; **Gerund**: Yendo / Siendo
Imperative: (tú) Ve / Sé; (ud.) Vaya / Sea; (nos.) Vayamos / Seamos; (vos.) Id / Sed; (uds.) Vayan / Sean

Crear and Creer

These two verbs have almost identical spelling. Because of the a⇔e exchange, there is a crossover between the **Present Indicative** and the **Present Subjunctive**, and in the **Imperative**:

Present Indicative

Crear		Creer	
Creo	**Creamos**	*Creo*	*Creemos*
Creas	**Creáis**	*Crees*	*Creéis*
Crea	**Crean**	*Cree*	*Creen*
Crea	**Crean**	*Cree*	*Creen*

Preterit Indicative

Crear: Creé, Creaste, Creó, Creamos, Creasteis, Crearon
Creer: Creí, Creíste, Creyó, Creímos, Creísteis, Creyeron

Imperfect Indicative

Crear: Creaba, Creabas, Creaba, Creábamos, Creabais, Creaban
Creer: Creía, Creías, Creía, Creíamos, Creíais, Creían

Present Subjunctive

Crear		Creer	
Cree	*Creemos*	Crea	**Creamos**
Crees	*Creéis*	Creas	**Creáis**
Cree	*Creen*	Crea	**Crean**
Cree	*Creen*	Crea	**Crean**

Imperfect Subjunctive

Crear: Creara, Crearas, Creara, Creáramos, Crearais, Crearan
Creer: Creyera, Creyeras, Creyera, Creyéramos, Creyerais, Creyeran

Participle: Creado / Creído; **Gerund**: Creando / Creyendo

Imperative: (tú) Crea / Cree; (ud.) Cree / Crea; (nos.) Creemos / Creamos; (vos.) Cread / Creed; (uds.) Creen / Crean

Sentar and Sentir

These two verbs have almost identical spelling. Because of the a⇔e exchange, there is a crossover between the **Present Indicative** and the **Present Subjunctive**, and in the **Imperative**:

Present Indicative

Sentar		Sentir	
Siento	Sentamos	Siento	Sentimos
Sientas	Sentáis	*Sientes*	Sentís
Sienta	**Sientan**	*Siente*	*Sienten*
Sienta	**Sientan**	*Siente*	*Sienten*

Preterit Indicative

Sentar: Senté, Sentaste, Sentó, Sentamos, Sentasteis, Sentaron
Sentir: Sentí, Sentiste, Sintió, Sentimos, Sentisteis, Sintieron

Imperfect Indicative

Sentar: Sentaba, Sentabas, Sentaba, Sentábamos, Sentabais, Sentaban
Sentir: Sentía, Sentías, Sentía, Sentíamos, Sentíais, Sentían

Present Subjunctive

Sentar		Sentir	
Siente	Sentemos	Sienta	Sintamos
Sientes	Sentéis	**Sientas**	Sintáis
Siente	*Sienten*	**Sienta**	**Sientan**
Siente	*Sienten*	**Sienta**	**Sientan**

Imperfect Subjunctive

Sentar: Sentara, Sentaras, Sentara, Sentáramos, Sentarais, Sentaran
Sentir: Sintiera, Sintieras, Sintiera, Sintiéramos, Sintierais, Sintieran

Participle: Sentado / Sentido; **Gerund**: Sentando / Sintiendo

**Imperative: (tú) Sienta / Siente; (ud.) Siente / Sienta;
(nos.) Sentemos / Sintamos; (vos.) Sentad / Sentid;
(uds.) Sienten / Sientan**

Quedar

Location
La escuela queda en la calle Escolar # 123.
(The school is in Scholar St. #123)

Commitment / Agreement
Quedamos en reunirnos el sábado a las 11:00 AM.
(We agreed to get together on Saturday at 11:00 AM)

Leftover
¿Quedó comida? (Was there any food left?)

Result of an action
La comida quedó muy buena. (The food was very good)

To stay
No voy a salir; voy a quedarme en mi casa.
(I'm not going out; I'm going to stay home)

To keep
Quedarse callado / Quedarse con algo
(To keep quiet / To keep something)

To fit
Esta camisa me queda bien; la voy a comprar.
(This shirt fits me well; I'm going to buy it)

Faltar

Any amount/quantity ahead or short
Faltan 5 millas para llegar. / Nos faltan 5 millas para llegar.
(There are 5 miles ahead to get there / We are 5 miles away to get there)

Faltan 5 minutos para terminar. (There are 5 minutes left to finish)

Me faltan $5 para la pizza grande. (I'm $5 short for the large pizza)

Failure / Lack
Falta de supervisión (Failure to supervise / Lack of supervision)

Falta de respeto (Lack of respect)

To be absent / To miss / To be missed
Faltar a una clase o reunión (To miss a class or meeting)

Me hace falta algo/alguien. (I miss something/someone)

"La hora", literally means "the hour", but it also refers to the time of the day. Therefore, "What time is it?" is "¿Qué hora es?".

Reloj = Clock or Watch
Hora = Hour; Minuto = Minute; Segundo = Second

Between 6:00 AM and 11:59 AM = La mañana (The morning).
12:00 PM = El mediodía ("The Midday": Noon).
Between 12:01 PM and 6:00 PM = La tarde (The afternoon).
Between 6:01 PM and 11:59 PM = La noche (The night).
12:00 AM = La medianoche (The Midnight).
Between 12:01 AM and 5:59 AM = La madrugada or La mañana (Early morning).

One O'clock = La una en punto
("La", in singular, refers to the hour: 1).
7:00 AM = Las siete de la mañana
("Las", in plural, refers to the hours: 7).
7:00 PM = Las siete de la noche.

When there are minutes after the hour, use "y (and)":
8:15 = Las ocho y quince (or: y cuarto = and a quarter).
8:30 = Las ocho y treinta (or: y media = and a half).

When there are minutes before the hour, use "menos (minus)":
8:45 = Las nueve menos quince (or: menos cuarto = minus a quarter).
Starting from the next hour, 9, subtracting the minutes.
(Or, go forward from the hour: Las ocho y cuarenta y cinco.)

Other than "quarters" and "halves", just add or subtract the minutes.

¿Qué hora es?
(The answer could be with singular "Es" or plural "Son".)
- Es la una y cuarenta. (It is 1:40)
- Son las dos menos veinte. ("2 minus 20" = 1:40 or 20 to 2)

Weather expressions use verbs like "<u>hacer</u>", "<u>estar</u>" and the <u>Present Progressive</u> tense. "El tiempo" (which literally means "the time") refers to the weather conditions on a specific day or short period, while "el clima" refers to the normal/general/all-year-round weather in a specific country, city or area.

<u>"Hacer"</u>
Hace calor (It is hot. Literally: "It makes heat")
Hace frío (It is cold. Literally: "It makes coldness")
Hace viento (It is windy. Literally: "It makes wind")

<u>"Estar" + Participle</u>
Está nublado (It is cloudy)
Está soleado (It is sunny)

<u>"Estar" + Gerund</u>
Está lloviendo (It is raining)
Está nevando (It is snowing)

Grados = Degrees
Celsius = Centígrado, Celsius
Fahrenheit = Fahrenheit

El tiempo hoy (Today's weather):

Está soleado/nublado y hace calor. (It is sunny/cloudy and it is hot)
Está lloviendo y hace viento. (It is raining and it is windy)
Hace frío y está nevando. (It is cold and it is snowing)
La temperatura es (de) 30 grados.* (The temperature is 30 degrees)
La temperatura está a/en 30 grados.*
(The temperature is at 30 degrees)
Hace 30 grados.* (It is 30 degrees. Literally: It makes 30 degrees)

*When referring to "el tiempo" (one specific day or short period), there are different ways to express the temperature, using "ser", "estar" or "hacer". But, when referring to the normal (in general) temperature in a region, "ser" is normally used instead (applying the main difference between "ser" = permanent, and "estar" = temporary):

La temperatura en Canadá es más baja que en Costa Rica.
(The temperature in Canada is lower than in Costa Rica)

De noche, la temperatura es de 20 grados, pero esta noche está a 40.
(At night, the temperature is 20 degrees, but tonight is at 40)

SOME COLLOQUIAL EXPRESSIONS
(& OTHER CONFUSING ONES)

Importar = To import / To matter, to care about, to be important.
No importa = It doesn't matter.
No me importa = I don't care (in Spanish it shows an attitude).
No importa qué = No matter what.
Lo que importa es... = What is important is.../The important thing is...

Ponerse... (viejo, gordo, etc) = To become...(old, fat, etc).
Ponerse/Amarrarse la soga al cuello = To tie the knot, to get married.
Ponerse a hacer algo = To start doing something.
Poner la mano en el fuego = To be very sure about something.
Poner "las cosas en su lugar" or "los puntos sobre las íes" = To straight things out, to clarify misunderstandings (but with an attitude).

Buen provecho = Enjoy your meal.
Aprovecharse de/Sacar provecho de=To take advantage of / To benefit from.
Aprovechar = To take/seize an opportunity.

Estar en onda = To be in tune, in sync, up to date.
Estar caliente = "To be hot". To be in trouble due to a bad action/behavior.
Estar como agua para chocolate = "To be like water for chocolate: hot". To be in trouble due to a bad action/behavior.
Estar limpio/pelado = "To be clean/peeled". To be out of money; broke.

Tener el agua hasta el cuello = "To have water up to your neck". To be in trouble, to have problems.
Tener la voz cantante = "To have the singing voice". To be the one saying what to do. To lead.
Tener en cuenta = To keep in mind. To take into account.

Quedarse con la cara larga = "To remain with a long face". To be deceived, short of words.

Quedarse pasmado = "To remain motionless". To be surprised, astonished, without reaction.

Pasársele la mano = To exceed the limit (doing something).

Pasarse de la raya = "To cross the line". To exceed the limit disrespectfully (behavior).

Pasar la papa caliente = "To pass the hot potato". To pass your problems to someone else.

Pasarse de listo = To outsmart someone (taking advantage).

A punto de caramelo = About to be done, almost done.

A punto de + V(inf) = About to + V(inf): "About to start".

Ya mismo + V(conj) = Will + V + soon: "Will start soon" / "About to start".

Hacerse pasar por... = To pretend to be...

Hacérsele la boca agua = To have a watery mouth, to crave.

Coger/Agarrar a uno con las manos en la masa = "To catch someone with his/her hands on the dough". To be caught in the act.

El tiempo de las vacas flacas = "Time of the skinny cows". Time of economic recession.

La cosa está floja = "The thing is weak". Things are slow.

La calle está dura = "The street is hard". It is tough out there.

Lucir = To show.

Lucirse = To show off.

Creerse lo último en la avenida = "To believe being the last thing on the avenue". To feel important/unique/superior. Stuck-up.

Romperse la cabeza = To break one's head (doing or figuring something out).

Saber más de la cuenta = To outsmart someone (taking advantage).

Salirse con la suya = "To come out with your own thing". To succeed persuading/taking advantage/achieving.

Salir por la puerta ancha = "To come out through the wide door". To be victorious, to end up in good shape.

Servirse con la cuchara ancha = "To serve oneself with the wide spoon". To take more than it is supposed.

Ser más viejo ...que el frío/...que Matusalén = "To be older ...than the cold/ ...than Matusalem". To be very old.

Celebrar/Recibir con bombos y platillos = "To celebrate/receive with drums and cymbals". To celebrate/welcome at max.

Oler mal/No oler bien = "To smell bad". When something does not seem to be right or there is a hidden agenda.

PREFIXES

I, In, Im (i, in, im) = contrary action or effect
   Ilícito, Inadecuado, Impaciencia (Illicit, Inadequate, Impatient)

Des (un, dis) = contrary action or effect
   Descubrir, Destapar, Deshacer (Discover, Uncover, Undo)

Sub (sub) = under, below
   Submarino (Submarine)

Super (super) = over, above
   Supersónico (Supersonic)

Hipo (hypo) = under, below
   Hipoglicemia, Hipopótamo (Hypoglycemia, Hippopotamus)

Hiper (hyper) = over, above
   Hipertensión (Hypertension)

Re (re)= repetition
   Reconstruir, Rehacer (Reconstruct, Redo)

Pos (post) = after
   Posponer, Posguerra (Postpone, Postwar)

Pro (pro) = instead, before, forward
   Pronombre, Prólogo, Promover (Pronoun, Prologue, Promote)

Ex (ex) = out, beyond
   Extraer, Exponer (Extract, Expose)

Co, Con, Com (co, con) = joined, partnered
    Coacusado, Confrontar (Codefendant, Confront)

Auto (auto) = self
    Automóvil, Autosuficiente (Automobile, Auto sufficient)

Inter (inter) = between, among
    Interracial, Interamericana (Interracial, Inter American)

Intra (intra) = inside
    Intravenoso (Intravenous)

Pan (pan) = all, totality
    Panamericano (Pan American)

-ción (tion) = to form nouns (verbal)
    Conjugación, Producción (Conjugation, Production)

-miento (ing) = to form nouns (v.) (action/effect)
    Levantamiento, Sentimiento (Lifting, Feeling)

-ísimo/a (N/A) = to form the superlative
    Malísimo, Buenísimo (Bad/Good in extreme)

-ismo (ism) = to form nouns as a system or field of study
    Socialismo, Capitalismo, Atletismo
    (Socialism, Capitalism, Athleticism)

-al (al) = to form nouns and adjectives
    Cultural, Neutral (Cultural, Neutral)

-ario/a (ary)= to form nouns and adjectives
    Fiduciario, Notario (Fiduciary, Notary)

-ista (ist) = to form nouns and adjectives
    Socialista, Capitalista (Socialist, Capitalist)

-or/a (er, or) = to form nouns and adjectives (v.)
    Corredor, Asesor (Runner, Advisor)

-ero/a (or) = to form nouns and adjectives
    Consejero, Traicionero (Advisor, Traitor)

-ante, ente (er, ent) = to form adjectives (v.)
    Caminante, Absorbente (Walker, Absorbent)

-able, ible (able, ible) = to form adjectives
>   Alcanzable, Reconocible, Infalible
>   (Achievable, Recognizable, Infallible)

-ístico/a (istic) = to form adj (belonging, relative)
>   Artístico, Característica (Artistic, Characteristic)

-mente (ly) = to form adverbs
>   Exitosamente, Fácilmente (Successfully, Easily)

-dad (ness, ility) = to form nouns (quality, characteristic)
>   Bondad, Maldad, Habilidad (Goodness, Badness, Ability)

English words with **"mm"** are written in Spanish with **"nm"**:

Immensity = Inmensidad
Immature = Inmaduro
Immediately = Inmediatamente
Immersion = Inmersión

English words with double consonants **"ss", "pp", "tt"** have a similar spelling in Spanish but with only one **"s", "p" or "t"**, respectively.

Possible = Posible
Possessive = Posesivo
(to) Possess = Poseer
Permission = Permiso
Mission = Misión
Admission = Admisión
Emission = Emisión

(to) Oppose = Oponer
(to) Appeal = Apelar
(to) Appear = Aparecer
Appearance = Apariencia
Apprentice = Aprendiz
Application = Aplicación. But, **Application form = Solicitud**.
(to) Apply = Aplicar. But, to **Apply for** a job/admission **= Solicitar**.

Attraction = Atracción
Attention = Atención

Made in the USA
Coppell, TX
03 August 2020

31908726R00081